THE CHEAPER THE CROOK, THE GAUDIER THE PATTER

THE CHEAPER THE CROOK, THE GAUDIER THE PATTER

Forgotten Hipster Lines,
Tough Guy Talk, and Jive Gems

ALAN AXELROD

Skyhorse Publishing

Skyhorse Publishing books may be purchased in bulk at special discounts for sales promotion, corporate gifts, fund-raising, or educational purposes. Special editions can also be created to specifications. For details, contact the Special Sales Department, Skyhorse Publishing, 307 West 36th Street, 11th Floor, New York, NY 10018 or info@skyhorsepublishing.com.

Skyhorse® and Skyhorse Publishing® are registered trademarks of Skyhorse Publishing, Inc.®, a Delaware corporation.

www.skyhorsepublishing.com

10 9 8 7 6 5 4 3 2 1

Library of Congress Cataloging-in-Publication Data is available on file.
ISBN: 978-1-61608-402-8

Printed in the United States of America

WILMER COOK: Keep on riding me and they're gonna be picking iron out of your liver.
SAM SPADE: The cheaper the crook, the gaudier the patter.
—***The Maltese Falcon*** (Warner Bros., 1941)

Contents

A Word or Two

ecember 22, 1944: the Battle of the Bulge. As the Nazi field commanders saw it, the Americans hadn't a prayer of holding on to the critical crossroads town of Bastogne, Belgium. They were cold, cut off, surrounded, and vastly outnumbered. Early in the morning, two German officers and a pair of noncoms, one of whom bore a white flag, approached Bastogne with a piece of paper. It was a surrender ultimatum. A somewhat-bewildered American officer carried the message to Brigadier General Anthony McAuliffe, acting commander of the 101st Airborne Division. As an airborne officer, McAuliffe believed that tight spots and desperate straits were a paratrooper's stock-in-trade. He therefore took it for granted that the officer was bringing him a *German* offer of surrender. When the messenger corrected this assumption, telling the general that it was the Germans who were demanding the surrender of the 101st, McAuliffe spat out something like a laugh.

"*Us* surrender? Aw, nuts!"

And when the messenger asked the general what reply he should make to the German envoys, McAuliffe told him that what he'd just said would do fine. McAuliffe scribbled "Nuts!" on a scrap of paper and handed it to the man.

The word spread rapidly across the European theater and was broadcast to the American home front. In the midst of the greatest crisis of the European campaign—a surprise German offensive that caught the Allies utterly flat-footed—a thrill of optimism and confidence in total victory suddenly blossomed. When Third U.S. Army CO General George S. Patton Jr. heard about McAuliffe's retort, he declared, "Any man who is that eloquent deserves to be rescued. We shall go right away."

The airborne commander's terse monosyllable was eloquent indeed, rich with the essence of smart-aleck vernacular defiance and contempt so typical of the American character, especially in the era of the Greatest Generation. "Nuts!" is one of the gems cut and polished during the Great Depression, World War I, and the postwar fifties, and now forgotten or in danger of being forgotten.

To lose the American eloquence of the tough guys and even-tougher broads, the hipsters, gunsels, gum-shoes, swabbies, Alibi Ikes, bad eggs, big butter-and-egg men, bimbos, drugstore cowboys, dishes, dreamboats, egg suckers, four-flushers, GI Joes, Jodies, kibitzers, knuckle busters, oomph girls, sad sacks, sweater girls, two-timers, vamps, visiting firemen, white-shoes, wood pushers, worrywarts, zhlubs, and zoot-suiters is a tragedy *The Cheaper the Crook, the Gaudier the Patter* is intended to prevent that.

You are about to embark on a seriously joyous mission to rescue the everyday vocabulary of the Greatest Generation, the rich American lexicon at its most pugnaciously, audaciously inventive.

ONE

Gumshoes, Gunsels, Mugs, and Molls

Notes from the Underworld

lley apple—A street cobblestone broken in half and carried in one's coat pocket to hurl as a missile. The phrase came into being during the 1930s, when bloody labor riots were commonplace in American cities. Strikers would bombard scabs, strike-breakers, Pinkerton men, and city cops with fragments of paving stone.

Artillery—What a gangster calls his handgun. Tough-guy alternatives from the 1920s through the 1950s include **bean shooter**, **boom stick**, **bullet dispenser**, **gat**, **gauge**, **four nickel**, **heat**, **heater** (see below), **jammy**, **rod**, **piece**, **roscoe**, **strap**, and **toaster**. Whatever it's called, a tough guy's gun fires a **pill** whenever he chooses to **burn powder**, **squirt metal**, or **throw lead** in order to **drill**, **fog**, **poke**, or **pop** someone.

Beef—A criminal charge or complaint. This was a term used by **hard-boiled** cops beginning in the 1950s and has stuck.

Q: "What's the **beef**, Sergeant?"

A: "Grand theft auto, Captain."

For a different kind of **beef**, see chapter 3, "Hipsters, Hepsters, Daddy-O's, and Zoot-Suiters."

Bent car—Stolen vehicle. The term was current by the 1940s and into the 1950s. The meaning may be an analogy with *crook* or *crooked* or may refer to the art of breaking into a vehicle without unduly damaging it—that is, bending rather than breaking.

Big House—The penitentiary. The phrase was being used by the mid-1800s and is often heard in gangster movies from the 1930s. **Big House** always means the state or federal penitentiary, as do the following terms from the heyday of organized crime: **can, pen, stir, slammer**, and (for cons whose tastes run droll) **college**. Terms such as **calaboose, clink, hoosegow**, and **pokey** refer exclusively to local and county jails. The expression **"to be sent up the river"** has its origin in sentencing to the Sing Sing Correctional Facility, opened in 1826 along the Hudson River in the town of Ossining, New York, which is located up the river from that perpetual font of criminality, New York City. Offenders convicted of major felonies in the city were often **sent**

up the river to Sing Sing; the phrase, however, may be applied to any penitentiary sentence.

Big sleep, the—Coined in 1939 by tough-guy novelist Raymond Chandler (1888–1959) as the title of his first novel featuring **hard-boiled** private eye Philip Marlowe, "the big sleep" caught on as a noir synonym for death (especially death by such unnatural causes as, say, a .38 slug through the aorta). For the title of a later Marlowe novel, Chandler coined another synonym for *mortality: The Long Good-Bye* (1953). In his 1971 foray into autobiography, *Fear and Loathing in Las Vegas: A Savage Journey to the Heart of the American Dream*, Gonzo journalist Hunter S. Thompson (1937–2005) gave a sly nod to Chandler when he referred to a drug-and-alcohol-induced fit of vomiting as "doing The Big Spit."

Bing—Solitary confinement, especially confinement to "the hole" as punishment for committing an infraction of prison rules. Among the non-incarcerated population circa 1930–1945, *bing* was slang for *crazy*; a con soon learned that solitary confinement drives some men nuts (*stir crazy*).

Bird—Mildly demeaning tough-guy synonym for *person* or *guy*, suggesting nonentity status. "Hey, any of you **birds** heard of a guy named Mel?"

More generally, since the 1800s, *bird* has served as a synonym for *person*—more specifically, a person perceived as strange or eccentric: "He's an odd **bird**, isn't he?" or "She's a sort of an artistic **bird**." Briefly, in the Swinging Sixties, **bird** was imported from England into the United States and used to describe a sexually attractive young woman; in the States, however, **chick** remained more popular. Also see **yardbird**.

Blip off—Kill. When gangsters of the 1920s and 1930s weren't busy rubbing out rivals, **stool pigeons**, and the like, they apparently passed the time inventing synonyms for *kill*. These included to **blow** (one) **down**, **bump off**, **chill off**, **clip**, **croak** (that is, "to *croak* the guy"), **cut down**, **daylight** (used as a verb, meaning to let in daylight by riddling with bullet holes or piercing with a knife: "Let's *daylight* da doity **mug**"), **drill**, **fog** (as a verb, meaning to shoot: "Go ahead, Lefty, *fog* 'em"), **ice** (another verb: "*Ice* the SOB"), **knock off**, (give one a case of) **lead poisoning**, **plug**, **poop**, **rub out**, **squirt metal into** (him), and **throw lead at** (him).

Once you plugged a **mug**, the proper thing to do was get him into a **Chicago overcoat** or a **wooden kimono** (coffin) and **plant** him (give him a proper funeral and a decent burial).

Boiler—Underworld slang for *car*. Heard in the 1920s, this was presumably either a reference to the tendency of radiators to boil over or an anachronistic nod to the Stanley Steamers, a series of steam-engine automobiles manufactured from 1902 until the company went belly-up in 1924. An alternative name for *car* was **bucket**; also see **short**.

Bootleg—Alcoholic beverages imported, manufactured, sold, and consumed in violation of Prohibition. A **bootlegger** was a purveyor of such illegal booze. Although the terms **bootleg** and **bootlegger** enjoyed a splendid renaissance during the Prohibition era of the 1920s and early 1930s, they had been coined back in the nineteenth century. The *Oxford English Dictionary* cites an 1889 *Omaha Herald* story about illegal liquor in Iowa (which had voted itself dry in 1882): "There is as much whisky consumed in Iowa now as there was before [the state amended its constitution to outlaw alcohol] . . . 'for medical purposes only,' and on the boot-leg plan."

The "boot-leg plan"? A boot leg is just what it says it is, the leg of a boot. Cowboys (and doubtless others) made a habit of storing various items in their boot legs, including knives, perhaps an extra sidearm, and almost certainly a flask of hooch. The idea of **bootlegging** as a form of smuggling stuck and was applied years later to the mechanics of evading the Eighteenth Amendment during Prohibition. Among the smuggling techniques was the practice of hiding a flask in a boot leg; some **flappers** adopted the fashion of wearing loose-cuffed Russian boots (or even unbuckled galoshes) and slipping a flask into the leg.

Box job—A safecracking caper, circa 1910–1950. A *safe* was called a **box**. To ambitious villains, a *vault* was nothing more than a big **box**. *But* note this hierarchy: a **box man** was a reliable journeyman safecracker, whereas a **can opener** was a small-time breaker of cheap home and office safes or strongboxes.

Brace (someone)—To confront harshly, or to shake down for money; to panhandle aggressively. In tough-talking police jargon, to **brace** a suspect is to interrogate him roughly and peremptorily. The word also applies to the approach of a confrontational or menacing panhandler, who gets in your face to ask for a handout and will not take no for an answer. In both senses, **brace** puts the focus on the "victim's" response to the exchange, which is to grimace, or "brace," as if pushed up against a wall (which might well be the case). Common from the 1930s and well into the 1950s, the term is antiquated today. "When I braced the **mug**, he sang like a **canary**."

Bracelets—Handcuffs. Used as a droll synonym since at least the nineteenth century, the term fell out of use by the 1950s.

Brodie, pull (or **do**, or **take**) **a**—Commit suicide, especially by jumping from a tall building or other structure. Through at least the 1940s, police officials informally reported a suicide by declaring that the "subject

pulled a Brodie." The expression originated in the claim of New York bartender Steve Brodie (1861–1901) that he had survived a leap off the Brooklyn Bridge on July 23, 1886. The problem? There were no witnesses. Nevertheless, local papers covered the unwitnessed feat extensively, giving Brodie the publicity he craved to accompany the opening of his On the Bowery tavern.

To **pull** (**take** or **do**) **a Brodie** was also used more generally to describe any accidental fall ("He cracked his skull **pulling a Brodie**") and, by extension, any notable fiasco or failure (a "flop"): "They spent a million bucks on the show, and it closed on opening night. **Took a Brodie**."

Bruno—An enforcer; **torpedo**. The term comes from the early days of the Italian-American domination of organized crime.

Bulge, to have the—To have an advantage or edge, as in "With **torpedoes** like that in his crew, Lefty's got **the bulge** in this city." **To have the bulge** is widely reported as gangster slang of the 1930s, but no authority has hazarded a guess as to origin. Reasonable surmises include an allusion to the bulge a holstered handgun creates in a suit coat, the bulge a fat bankroll creates in a pocket, or maybe even the bulge evident in the trouser front of an especially well-endowed man.

Bull—Primarily, a prison guard; secondarily, a cop. Also used to refer to a plainclothes railroad policeman whose function was mainly to prevent theft in rail yards and to throw free-riding hobos out of boxcars (see **cinder bull**). Although this term is closely associated with gangster-era toughs—and especially penitentiary inmates—**bull** had been used as a synonym for any peace officer or official of law enforcement since the 1600s.

During the 1930s through the early 1940s, a **bull buster** was a man who assaulted a police officer or other law enforcement official, and to be **bull simple** was to have a chronic and irrational fear of the police. **Fresh bull** was the term used for a particular though rare annoyance: the straight-arrow, honest, incorruptible cop.

Bull's wool—Stolen merchandise. The phrase first appeared in print in 1945, but may be related to the earlier **bull wool**, meaning anything *cheap*.

Bus—As used by 1930s-era gangsters, a large sedan (in contrast to a coupe). During the 1920s and 1930s, automobiles rose to critical importance in the successful commission of crimes ranging from bank robbery to bootlegging. Small and fast was always good for getaways, but *big* and fast was best for making a strong impression.

Button man—Hired killer; professional gangland assassin; more recently, a rank-and-file mafioso (a "soldier"). The term has been around since the 1920s and seems to have denoted a professional killer from then through the 1930s. By the post–World War II era, **button man** had been appropriated by the Mafia and meant a Mob "soldier." Some authorities believe that the expression was a reference to hotel bellhops, whose uniforms typically featured many shiny buttons and whose vocation it was to do the bidding of others without asking questions or telling tales; however, the **button men** themselves understood their function as simply this: to "push the button on a guy" (that is, kill) whenever so ordered.

Buttons—Police, either an individual officer or police in general (i.e., "the cops"). In many municipalities from about 1920 into the 1950s, large brass buttons were highly conspicuous features of police uniforms. Sometimes, as with the NYPD, the buttons were arranged in double-breasted tunic style, converging toward the hem of the blouse. In fact, the only thing more conspicuous than the uniform buttons was the badge, derisively referred to as a **buzzer**, as if it were inviting a door-buzzer push. "Look, **buttons**, you got nuthin' on me."

Can and **can house**—Prison and bordello, respectively. Presumably, **can house** is a variation on *cathouse*, a synonym for *bordello* that dates from the end of the nineteenth century and is founded on *cat* as a synonym for both *prostitute* and *vulva* (*pussy*).

Canary—A female singer from the swing or big band era (1930s–early 1950s); also, in an underworld context, an informant, a snitch. In the first sense, the word seems to have been borrowed by white musicians from African American slang, where it was applied to any songstress. As used by white musicians, however, **canary** was usually limited to female singers who fronted swing bands and other big bands, not nightclub or cabaret singers, who were typically accompanied by a piano only. Variations include **thrush** and **warbler**. In *All Through the Night* (1941), professional gambler Gloves Donahue (played by Humphrey Bogart) says of singer Leda Hamilton (played by Kaaren Verne), "That **canary**'s in a jam."

In the second sense, **canary** emerged as an ironic alternative to the more established term **stool pigeon** to describe one who snitches or informs on one's fellow criminals. **Stool pigeon** appeared in the early 1800s and is derived from a hunter's practice of fastening a pigeon to a stool as a decoy to attract game. "He was convicted when his accomplice sang like a **canary**."

Carry a flag—Assume an alias and operate under it; also, to travel incognito. This underworld term of art may have derived from "false flag operation," a covert military action carried out by one nation but made to look like the work of another; "false flag" is a phrase that has been in use since at least the eighteenth century and comes from the practice of covertly sailing a warship under another nation's flag.

Cellar smeller—The **bootlegger**'s best friend, a hard drinker; also, an alcoholic, a drunkard. The phrase was popular during Prohibition.

Cheaters—Sunglasses. Since the early 1900s, **cheaters** has been slang for *eyeglasses*, and the term is still occasionally used in this way, mostly by very senior senior citizens or by younger people in a lame effort at humor. In the underworld of the 1920s through the 1940s, and perhaps into the 1950s, **cheaters** generally connoted sunglasses rather than corrective lenses, and they were used less to keep the sun out of one's eyes than to disguise one's identity. **Cheaters** also sometimes referred to a marked deck of cards.

Chicago lightning and **Chicago overcoat**—*Gunfire* and *coffin*, respectively. Prohibition, which spanned 1919 to 1933, transformed the United States into precisely what President Woodrow Wilson, who was opposed to the passage and ratification of the Eighteenth Amendment outlawing liquor, warned it would become: a nation of outlaws. And in no American city were the outlaws more numerous, more violent, and more successful than in Chicago, whose government was openly in the bag and exuberantly on the take. During the Roaring Twenties, therefore, the Windy City became the archetype of all things brazenly criminal, and the world began to speak of **Chicago lightning** instead of *gunfire* and a **Chicago overcoat** rather than a *coffin*.

Chinese angle—A strange, unexpected twist; a surprising, very clever approach, with the strong implication of illegality. Even as late as the 1920s, the Chinese were widely regarded by Westerners as inscrutable people speaking an indecipherable language and operating from unfathomable motives. Thus a **Chinese angle** was a mystery, a complex bit of chicanery beyond the comprehension of the average Joe. It is conceivable that the expression owes a debt to the British game of cricket, in which "Chinese cut" is a familiar term for what is technically called an "inside edge," a subtle deviation of the ball off the edge of the bat that barely misses hitting the wicket. In other words, "Chinese cut" describes a remarkably well-played, skillfully controlled hit.

Chopper and **chopper squad**—Respectively, machine (Tommy) gun and a group of men who wield them. The iconic weapon of the American gangster era between the world wars was the Thompson submachine gun, or Tommy gun, called "the gun that made the twenties roar."

The weapon was invented during World War I by retired U.S. Army colonel and Remington Arms Company engineer John T. Thompson (1860–1940), but was not ready for manufacture before 1919, a year after the war ended. As a "submachine" gun, the Thompson combined the fully automatic fire of a standard machine gun with the portability of a cartridge-loaded pistol. The weapon's ability to fire between 600 and 1,200 rounds per minute (depending on the model) prompted soldiers to call it a "trench broom" or "trench sweeper." Contrary to urban myth, gangsters did not acquire the Tommy gun in bulk via post–World War I army surplus sales, but the weapon was certainly widely available to civilians—indeed, to anyone who ponied up the cash to buy it. It soon became known as the **Chicago Piano**, the **Chicago Typewriter**, and the **chopper**. Its popularity among gangsters was sufficiently widespread to prompt passage of the National Firearms Act by the United States Congress in 1934. The new law did not prohibit civilian sales of the Thompson, but it did require all fully-automatic firearms to be registered with the federal government through the agency that later became the Bureau of Alcohol, Tobacco, Firearms and Explosives (ATF).

It was a **chopper squad** that perpetrated the infamous St. Valentine's Day Massacre of February 14, 1929, in Chicago, when four Tommy gun–wielding **button men** (presumably in the employ of Al Capone) lined up six members of Bugs Moran's North Side Gang (plus another victim) against a wall and mowed them down.

Cinder bull—A **railroad dick** (railroad detective). Cinders were intimately associated with railroads during the age of coal-burning steam locomotives and were often the principal constituent of the roadbed on which the tracks were laid; hence the **cinder** adjective modifying **bull**.

Claw—To arrest. Not as popular or as enduring a term as **collar**, **claw** is, if anything, even more vividly descriptive of the act.

Daylight—Used as a verb, meaning to let in the daylight—that is, to shoot someone, putting a hole or holes in him that will let the daylight shine through. This is hardcore tough-guy talk from the 1940s: "Daylight the SOB! Drill 'im good!"

Dick—Detective, especially a private detective (**private dick**). Specialized **dicks** include the **store dick** (store detective, who works in plainclothes looking for shoplifters), **house dick** (plainclothes security officer employed by a hotel), and **railroad dick** (plainclothes railroad security officer, whose principal duty is throwing hobos off freight trains; also called a **cinder bull**). **Dick** is ostensibly a shortened form of *detective*, but the duplication of the familiar word referring to the penis as well as to a despised person ("He's a real **dick**") is hardly coincidental. As a synonym for *detective*, **dick** has been in use since the early nineteenth century.

Dingus—An unspecified (perhaps unspecifiable) thing or object. **Dingus** was sometimes used to refer to a stolen item, the vagueness of the term intended to avoid the potential self-incrimination of actually describing the loot. In Dashiell Hammett's classic *The Maltese Falcon*, **hard-boiled** detective Sam Spade repeatedly refers to the apparently priceless falcon statuette—the object of a multiply fatal quest—as "the **dingus**." The word is almost certainly derived from the German *Ding* or the Dutch *dinges*, both of which mean "thing."

Do my time or **do my bit**—Serve my prison sentence. The rise of organized crime beginning in the 1920s and extending into the present day virtually ensured that one or more substantial prison sentences would be part of any career criminal's résumé. Accordingly, convicts sought to express their sentence in business-as-usual terms and therefore spoke of **doing my time** or having to **do my bit.** "Good-bye, Ma. I'll see you after I **do my bit.**"

Drop the dime—or **nickel**—(on someone)—Incriminate; snitch to police. In the heyday of the urban gangster, the 1930s, a payphone call cost a nickel. From the mid-1950s through most of the 1970s, it was a dime. Informing on someone to the police was depicted as making an anonymous phone call—dropping (depending on the decade) a nickel or a dime into the coin slot. "The filthy stoolie **dropped the dime** on me!"

Dropper—A hired killer. The business of a hired gun was to make a target fall—to drop him. Thus the name of a profession was born in the 1930s or 1940s. See also **torpedo**.

Dumb gat—A stolen gun rendered untraceable by having its serial numbers filed off. Handguns have long borne serial numbers, largely as an aid to identifying stolen weapons. With the rise of organized crime in the 1920s and 1930s, sophisticated criminals made it a practice to file the serial numbers off of the weapons they used. In this way, the gun (**gat**), having been rendered mute (**dumb**), could no longer "testify" to the authorities.

Dummy up—The proper response to police interrogation, i.e., total silence. Among figures of organized crime, those most respected—the **stand-up guys**—commanded the fortitude to **dummy up** under even the harshest **third degree** interrogation.

Earwigging—Eavesdropping; also, relentlessly talking someone into doing something. An earwig, of the order Dermaptera, is a small insect that spends the daylight hours in tight, small, dark spaces, venturing out only at night. Although such environments might well include the human ear, the belief that earwigs enter the ear in order to burrow into the brain for the purpose of laying their eggs is an old wives' tale that goes back at least as far as the Middle Ages. The insect's name is derived from Old English *eare* (ear) + *wicga* (insect), and the Old English language was in use from roughly the fifth through the eleventh centuries. Although some authorities believe **earwigging** was a common gangster-era synonym for eavesdropping and was used at least as early as the 1930s, others assert that it was actually invented by the comedians of *The Goon Squad,* a 1950s BBC comic radio show that was the ancestor of *Monty Python's Flying Circus.*

The other sense of **earwigging**, relentlessly talking someone into doing something, has been recorded at least as early as the 1920s.

Electric cure—Death by electric chair. By the 1930s, electrocution was the most common method of execution in the United States. Widely touted as "humane," the electric chair sometimes took up to eight minutes to kill a person, sometimes required multiple applications of current, sometimes set hair and body on fire, and sometimes visibly ruptured multiple blood vessels. Many western American states favored hanging (**the Jump**), and California, like Nevada, used the gas chamber (the agent of death being cyanide vapor, nicknamed **Nevada gas**). Note that from the last quarter of the nineteenth century through the first half of the twentieth, a host of patent medical devices were marketed as "electric cures," intended to treat everything from nervous disorders to cancer. Like many other articles of tough-guy slang, **electric cure** (meaning electric chair) was a piece of **hard-boiled** irony. The **hot seat** or **burner** (two more nicknames) was the sovereign cure for what ailed the individual and society alike.

Fakealoo (or **fake aloo**) **artist**—Con man. During the 1920s to 1930s, a **fakealoo** (or **fake aloo**) was a fabricated hardluck story, and a **fakealoo artist** was a grifter who, armed with a compelling hard-luck story, swindled the gullible out of money. The origin of the term is unknown, though we might note the similarity to *switcheroo*, which is still sometimes used to describe scams in which something of great value is shown to a buyer but something else of little value is actually delivered.

Frame-up—This Americanism, meaning to give false testimony or fabricate evidence to fraudulently prove someone guilty of a crime, has been around since the early 1900s. Although born in the USA it is most likely derived from *frame* as encountered in British common law, meaning to put someone "in a [picture] frame of suspicion." The word was used extensively in American popular fiction and film during the 1930s and 1940s, as, for example, in the 1946 film noir *The Dark Corner,* in which ex-con turned private detective Bradford Galt (played by Mark Stevens) laments to his wisecracking secretary Kathleen (Lucille Ball), "I can be framed easier than Whistler's Mother."

George—Excellent ("That arrangement is **George** with me, Lefty."); also reported as a verb, meaning to know or to be wise to ("Stop talking already. I **George** every one of your excuses by heart."). In both senses, the word was associated with the U.S. underworld and was reported as early as 1930. In British English, the word was used as a synonym for *defecate*—but that sense was not recorded until 1959.

Gumshoe—A detective. Plainclothes police officers were supposed to blend in with the citizens and suspects among whom they mingled during investigations. One thing, however, often gave them away. Their rubber-soled shoes (called **gumshoes** in the early twentieth century) were the sign of a man whose job kept him on his feet for long hours. The word also suggests a dogged investigator who nevertheless is not overly bright.

Gunsel—An armed hood. During the gangster era of the 1930s and 1940s, a **gunsel** was a low-level gunman in the service of a crime boss. The boss was the brains, the **gunsel** the muscle. Never flattering, the word was further tainted by an earlier meaning derived from hobo and prison culture, in which a **gunsel** was a young man or youth targeted by an older man for sex. Dashiell Hammett's **hard-boiled** private detective Sam Spade means to be insulting when he suggests setting up the sadistic little gangster Wilmer Cook (played by Elisha Cook Jr. in the 1941 film version of Hammett's *The Maltese Falcon*) as a fall guy. "Give 'em the **gunsel**," Spade says.

Hard-boiled—Tough; used to describe a genre of popular detective fiction rife with violence and sex, in which crimes are solved by a steely, unsentimental **private eye**. **Hard-boiled** is a brilliant slang understatement intended as an exact synonym for *tough*. It is derived from the fact that hard-boiling an egg produces a tough white encasing a hard yolk, as opposed to soft boiling, which yields a soft, runny white and yolk. The term was current in the mid-1920s when writer Carroll John Daly (1889–1958) began turning out a series of popular private crime novels in which the protagonists, all private detectives, were described as "**hard-boiled**." Critics and others applied the term to the even more popular noir fiction of Dashiell Hammett (1894–1961) and Raymond Chandler (1888–1959). Very early on, the word's utility was expanded to describe anything or anyone possessing the tough character or appearance of a **hard-boiled** detective; for example, in *This Side of Paradise* (1920), F. Scott Fitzgerald describes a "rather hard-boiled painting that hangs in Father's office."

Harlem sunset—A mortal wound inflicted by knife. By the 1910s and '20s, Manhattan's Harlem neighborhood had become famous as the cultural capital of black

America—scene of a remarkable literary and artistic flowering dubbed "the Harlem Renaissance"—and as a nexus of urban violence, at least as the white American press saw it. Accurately or not, reporters noted that street disputes often escalated into knife fights and any resulting wound, if fatal, came to be called a **Harlem sunset**.

Heater—Handgun. The term was in use by the 1930s, especially among gangsters and gangster wannabes, but it was popularized by Richard Wright's novel *Native Son*, which made a sensation in 1940 as the story of Bigger Thomas, a young African American living on Chicago's South Side, who accidentally kills a white woman and then deliberately rapes and kills his girlfriend. **Heaters** abound in Bigger's ghetto world, and they soon appeared in an abundance of tough-guy films. In one of these, *Kansas City Confidential* (1952), out-of-work trucker Joe Rolfe (played by John Payne) responds to a cop during a brutal **third degree** with "What makes a two-bit heel like you think a **heater** would give him an edge over me?" (See also **artillery** above.)

Jack—As a noun, money, cash; as a verb, to steal. From at least 1890, **jack** was a synonym for money, mainly used in the underworld; presumably, there is a connection with *jackpot*. As a synonym for *steal*, **jack** was first noted in 1930 and is presumably a shortened version of *hijack*.

Kisser—Mouth. The origin of this word almost certainly predates its tough-guy heyday in the 1930s and 1940s, and was probably current among prizefighters by the mid- to late nineteenth century to describe the mouth as a prime target for a punch, as in "Pow! Right in the **kisser**."

Kneecapping—A deliberate knee wound inflicted with a pipe, baseball bat, or firearm, typically as a form of gangland retaliation short of murder or as a form of intimidation, often used to "encourage" regular payment of loan shark loans. Although **kneecapping** is most closely associated with organized crime in the United States, it was, and is, widely practiced by paramilitary terrorist groups worldwide, most infamously by Italian fascists during the 1920s and by Irish and Northern Irish independence groups.

Moll—A criminal's girlfriend or female accomplice. The word was used mainly by the press in reporting gangster stories during the 1920s and faded out by the following decade; it dates, however, from eighteenth-century London, in which a **moll** was any lower-class woman or, more specifically, a prostitute (hence the eponymous heroine of Daniel Defoe's 1722 novel, *Moll Flanders*). In origin, **moll** is short for *Molly*, which is itself a diminutive of *Mary*. A gangster-era variant of **moll** is **gun moll**, used mainly by journalists reporting crime than by the criminals themselves. Despite the obvious implication of gun (***gun* moll** = *gun*woman), the *gun* part of the phrase is probably derived from the Yiddish word *gonif*, meaning "thief," rather than from the firearm.

Mug—One of the most versatile words in the tough guy's lexicon, **mug** can be a noun or a verb and can mean any of the following: the face; police photograph of an arrestee (**mug** shot); to make a police photo of an arrestee ("**Mug** him, Sergeant"); to make grotesque or exaggerated facial expressions, usually for comic effect ("Sonny, don't **mug** for the camera like that!"); a tough guy, usually a thug ("He's one of Capone's **mugs**, outta Chicago"); and to assault and rob someone ("It's a tough neighborhood, so you're liable to get mugged"). Although the word, in all its senses, is so closely identified with the gangster era that we would assume it was born of that time, **mug** is actually of much older lineage. The word has meant *face* since at least the early eighteenth century, when it reflected the popularity of putting faces—often comically grotesque faces—on drinking mugs. The sense of **mug** as a grotesque or comical grimace dates at least from the early nineteenth century, when it was used in the theater to describe the exaggerated facial expressions that go along with bad acting.

Private eye—A private investigator, often abbreviated as *PI* from which the *eye* element is derived. The term *private investigator* rapidly evolved from *private detective,* which became current in the United States by 1850, when Scots immigrant Allan J. Pinkerton founded his famed Pinkerton's Detective Agency. The progression from *private investigator*—PI—to *private eye* was doubtless accelerated by the Pinkerton trademark, a wide-open eye over the motto "We Never Sleep."

From the 1930s through the 1950s, **hard-boiled** detective fiction and movies made the term **private eye** more popular than *private detective* or *private investigator*. Sometimes, the phrase was shortened to the single word **eye**. The alternative, **private dick**, was also frequently used during this period, **dick** being short for *detective*. The term was derived from *house detective* (familiarly called the **house dick**), the job title for plainclothes private security personnel employed by hotels in the early twentieth century to address any "trouble" with or among guests without involving the city police and consequent negative publicity.

Stand-up guy—In organized crime, a reliable partner or accomplice, one who can be trusted not to cave in under the **third degree**. From the 1950s on, the phrase became increasingly associated with the Mafia, in which a **stand-up guy** is one who will do anything necessary for the good of his "crew" or "family." The earliest recorded use of the phrase is reported from a story that appeared in *The Charleroi Mail* (Pennsylvania) in

April 1935: " . . . he seems to be a **stand up** guy and loy-
alty, with him, seems to be less a virtue than obsession."

Stool pigeon—Police informant; snitch. Also called
a **stoolie**, **stool pigeon** has proved to be a very durable
term, with an origin in the early nineteenth century
and frequently encountered in tough-guy fiction and
film from the 1930s on. The phrase is derived from the
hunter's practice of fastening a pigeon (or other bird) to a
wooden stool and setting it out as a decoy to attract game
birds or game animals. The analogy is therefore to bait so
as to draw the target to the hunter. Not only is the phrase
stool pigeon derisive, it is also predictive of the **stoolie**'s
fate. Live bait rarely stays alive for long.

Other terms commonly employed in the realm of
gangsters to describe informants include the following:

- **rat** (also **rat fink**): Some believe this is a rhyming
  reference to *Pink*erton operatives, who operated as
  plainclothes infiltrators to inform on strike organ-
  izers in the nineteenth and early twentieth century.
- **Grass** (or **supergrass**): Another instance of rhyming
  slang: short for *grasshopper*, which rhymes with
  copper (cop, or police officer) or perhaps with *shopper*

(one who *shops*—betrays, turns in—a partner in crime).

- **Narc:** An undercover police officer who infiltrates a narcotics ring. This may be different in origin from **nark**, believed to derive from *nak*, a Romany word for "nose," or from the French *narquois*, meaning "cunning and deceitful."
- **Rat:** one who rats another out
- **Snitch**
- **Snout** or **nose**
- **Squealer:** who *squeals* to authorities
  See also **drop the dime**—or **nickel**—(on someone).

Tag—An arrest warrant. The underworld currency of the term in 1930s is attested to by its use in more than one Raymond Chandler novel. **Private eye** Philip Marlowe asks, "Is there a **tag** out for me?"

Ten-four—Police radio "ten code" meaning "Message received OK." In the early days of mobile communication, when "modern" police cruisers were called "radio cars," police officers and their dispatchers relied on the so-called ten code, in which frequently used expressions were reduced for clarity to numbers beginning with ten. As a public service, we now bring you the entire standard ten code, circa 1950:

10-1: Receiving poorly

10-2: Receiving OK

10-4: Message received OK

10-5: Relay to

10-7: Out of service at

10-7B: Out of service, personal

10-70D: Off duty

10-8: In service

10-9: Repeat

10-10: Out of service at home

10-12: Visitors or officials present

10-13: Weather and road conditions

10-14: Escort

10-14F: Funeral detail

10-15: Have prisoner in custody

10-16: Pick up

10-19: Return to station

10-20: Location

10-21: Phone your office

10-21A: Phone my home, my ETA is

10-21B: Phone your home

10-21R: Phone radio

10-22: Cancel

10-23: Standby

10-25: Do you have contact with

10-28: Registration

10-29: Check for wanted

10-32: Drowning

10-33: Alarm sounding

10-34: Open door

10-35: Open window

10-39: Status of

10-40: Is available for phone call

10-45: Ambulance, injured

10-46: Ambulance, sick

10-49: Proceed to

10-50: Obtain a report

10-51: Drunk

10-52: Resuscitator

10-53: Man down

10-54: Possible dead body

10-55: Coroner's case

10-56: Suicide

10-56A: Attempted suicide

10-57: Firearms discharged

10-58: Garbage complaint

10-59: Malicious mischief

10-62: Meet the citizen

10-65: Missing person

10-66: Suspicious person

10-67: Person calling for help

10-70: Prowler

10-71: Shooting

10-72: Knifing

10-73: How do you receive?

10-80: Explosion

10-86: Any traffic for

10-87: Meet officer

10-91: Stray animal

10-91A: Vicious animal

10-91B: Noisy animal

10-91C: Injured animal

10-91D: Dead animal

10-91F: Animal bite

10-911H: Stray horse

10-97: Arrived at the scene

10-98: Finished with last assignment

11-24: Abandoned vehicle

11-26: Abandoned bicycle

11-54: Suspicious vehicle

11-79: Accident, ambulance en route

11-80: Accident, major injury

11-81: Accident, minor injury

11-82: Accident, property damage

11-83: Accident, no detail

11-84: Traffic control

11-96: Leaving vehicle to investigate an auto; if not heard from in 10 minutes, dispatch cover

The phrase **ten-four**—signifying "message received," "I understand," or "I agree"—was popularized by the television show *Highway Patrol*, which aired for 156 episodes from 1956 to 1959 and starred consummately surly and mildly overweight tough-cop actor Broderick Crawford (1911–1986). Dialogue throughout the series was heavily peppered with ten-code—especially **ten-four**—which Crawford growled into the mike of his radio car.

Three hots and a cot—The glass-half-full point of view on a prison sentence. Sure, doing time means confinement, no dames, hard labor, and maybe even a shiv in the back, but at least you get three hot meals a day and a place to sleep. The phrase has been around at least since the 1930s.

Throw the book at you (**him**, **them**, etc.)—To level against a defendant every conceivable charge for an offense or set of offenses, or to mete out the severest

penalty. Current from at least as early as the 1920s, the expression combines the idea of a physical assault with a hurled missile and the metaphorical meaning of such an assault: to be charged with as many violations of *the book* (of laws) as possible.

Defendant: "Your Honor, I'm just a victim of circumstance . . ."

Judge: "I'm tired of your excuses. This time, I intend to **throw the book at you** and put you away for a long, long time."

Throw, **throwdown**, or **throw-down**—A handgun planted (thrown down) by police to incriminate a suspect or to justify a shooting by officers. The term was recorded in the 1950s and continues to be in use today. Some cops would carry an extra handgun to plant as evidence, either to fabricate probable cause for an arrest or to justify shooting an unarmed suspect.

Torpedo—Hired thug; an enforcer, though not necessarily a killer. A **torpedo** was mob "**muscle**" hired to intimidate a rival or punish the uncooperative. Unlike a **dropper**, the **torpedo** was not necessarily a paid assassin. His work might consist of no more than issuing a savage beating. On the other hand, once violence was called for, it could be difficult to modulate. The term comes from the naval weapon, fired on command from a ship or submarine—a projection of destructive power remote from the individual who gave the order for its use. "Al Capone started out as a **torpedo** for Johnny Torrio."

Short eyes—Prison term for a convict incarcerated for child molestation. This sense of the word came into use by the 1950s. **Short eyes** is a term used by convicts to describe other convicts. Cops, in the 1940s and 1950s, called pedophiles **kiddie rapers.** "He's no good. Got **short eyes**. They put him away on a **kiddie raper beef**."

Take (someone) **downtown**—Arrest or detain for questioning at police headquarters. The expression was born of an era in which the urban police headquarters building was inevitably downtown. The difference between getting hauled into the precinct and being taken downtown was one of degree: the local precinct was fine for misdemeanor issues, but **downtown** was the place to deal with serious criminals. Go there, and you were in for the **third degree**.

Take (someone) **for a ride**—To abduct, murder, and dispose of the body, typically in a remote place, gangster-style. To be **taken for a ride** was no picnic in the 1920s and 1930s, since it was a euphemism for a gangland execution and disposal of remains. The victim was abducted, forced into a car (usually a large black sedan, known as a **bus**), driven to a secluded place, and dispatched with extreme prejudice. Sometimes the execution was relatively merciful: a bullet to the back of the head. Sometimes it was more in the nature of torture, in which case the mutilated corpse was left where it would be found and duly interpreted as a message to rivals, the authorities, or others. Informants and **stool pigeons** were frequent victims. The corpse of the informant, called a **rat**, would often be left with an actual dead rat shoved into its mouth.

Third degree, the—A rigorous, even brutal police interrogation. This synonym for an extreme interrogation has been in use at least since 1900, as attested to by an article in *Everybody's Magazine* that year. The origin of the phrase is obscure, but there are two leading theories as to its etymology. In 1910, Richard Sylvester, then president of the International Association of Chiefs of Police, sought to define **the third degree** without the emotional connotation of brutality by saying that "first degree" referred to the arrest of a suspect, "second degree" to detention or confinement, and "third degree" to interrogation. **The third degree** was thus nothing more than a routine step in a routine progression. The problem with this explanation is that the word *degree* does not imply the stages of a process, as, for example, the word *step* would; therefore, *degree* has no place in this description of a progression. Moreover, legal texts make no reference to the stages of arrest, detention, and interrogation as *degrees.* Perhaps more plausible is an analogy with the three basic degrees of Freemasonry. A Mason enters the Craft as Entered Apprentice (he is a First Degree Mason), progresses to the Second Degree, called Fellowcraft, and is eventually admitted to the Third Degree, Master Mason. The initiation into the Third Degree is shrouded in secrecy (at least theoretically, for many books have been written about it) and involves a variety of symbolic but dramatic physical threats. Both physically and psychologically, the ritual of admission to the Third Degree is more extreme than for the first two degrees. The Freemason etymology for harsh interrogation seems all the more plausible when one considers that in the United States at the turn of the nineteenth century, most towns had at least one Masonic Lodge and membership in the Masons was widespread, familiar, yet, in some quarters, controversial.

Although in use by the very beginning of the twentieth century, **the third degree** became especially prominent beginning in 1931, when President Herbert Hoover created the Wickersham Commission (headed by former U.S. Attorney General George W. Wickersham) to investigate the causes of criminal activity and make public policy recommendations concerning its eradication. The commission concluded (among many other things) that application of the **third degree**— which is defined as "the inflicting of pain, physical or mental, to extract confessions or statements"—was "widespread throughout the country."

Vig—Short for *vigorish,* a commission charged by a bookie; or the interest on a loan shark loan. The term seems to have come about with the rise of the Jewish underworld beginning in the 1920s and the emergence of such figures as "professional gambler" Arnold Rothstein (1882–1928) and organized crime organizer Meyer Lansky (1902–1983). *Vigorish* is a Yiddish word that originated in the Russian word *vyigrysh*, meaning "winnings" in the sense of "gambling proceeds." In the case of a loan shark loan, the **vig** is a minimum weekly payment made (as interest continues to accrue) until the loan is paid off. The **vig** never reduces the principal, and failure to meet a **vig** payment may result in a **kneecapping** or worse.

Whodunit—Mystery/detective novel or movie. This familiar shorthand for a mystery or detective story did not surface until the 1930s. The implication is of a mystery story with a conventional or formulaic plot rather than a true-to-life tale of crime.

Yardbird—Primarily, a convict, especially in a penitentiary; secondarily, a military recruit or a stockade (military jail) inmate. Sometimes also applied to a derelict or bum. **Bird** was popular slang for *person*, roughly the more demeaning equivalent of *guy*, from the 1930s well into the 1950s. The use of **yardbird** more or less corresponds to this period and suggests birds in out-door confinement, such as the milling occupants of a prison exercise yard. Some authorities believe the word, as applied to convicts seen in a prison yard or military recruits "policing" (cleaning up) an assigned outdoor area, implies a resemblance to the milling and pecking behavior of pigeons in an urban space.

Yegg—A bad or sinister man, a criminal type. The *Oxford English Dictionary* finds the earliest print use of **yegg** in a *New-York Evening Post* article from 1903, though many authorities believe the word was in wide circulation during the nineteenth century. Early in the twentieth century, **yegg** described a burglar and, often even more specifically, a safecracker. By the 1930s (after which the use of the word faded away), **yegg** was applied to any criminal type or mean or bad man living on the edge of the law. As for the word's origin, some believe that a certain John Yegg was a Swedish-born tramp who cracked safes in California during the late nineteenth century. Other authorities trace the word to the German *Jäger* (hunter), suggesting a link between the profession of itinerant burglar and a catch-as-catch-can hunter. Neither of these etymologies is widely considered definitive or even very plausible, so the origin of **yegg** remains a mystery.

You can't make an omelet without breaking eggs—The end justifies the means. As Shakespeare wrote in *The Merchant of Venice*, "To do a great right, do a little wrong." Or, as Al Capone put it, "You can get much farther with a kind word and a gun than you can with a kind word alone." Improbable though it seems, scholars have traced the origin of the expression to Vladimir I. Lenin, who broke more than a few eggs (including some by Fabergé) to pull off the Bolshevik Revolution.

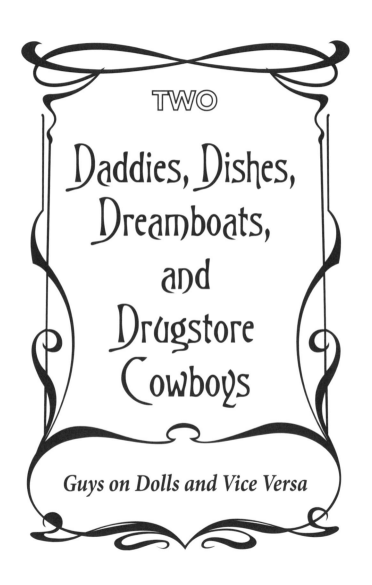

TWO

Daddies, Dishes, Dreamboats, and Drugstore Cowboys

Guys on Dolls and Vice Versa

ll dressed up and (or **with**) **no place to go**—Ready for a good time, but no takers or no venue. The origin is a song by one Raymond Hitchcock from something like 1915. It was often used by a gal or a guy who'd been stood up for a date. "Edna says she forgot that she has to **wash her hair** tonight. Looks like I'm **all dressed up with no place to go.**"

All show and no go—Flirtatious, flashy, florid, but flaccid. Used by a disappointed **flapper** to describe a disappointing night. "I thought I'd be worn out this morning, but he turned out to be **all show and no go.**"

All that meat and no potatoes!—A **hipster**'s paean to a well-built woman. Typically, this was spoken loudly enough to be heard by the object of admiration, and although it is clearly more genteel than **built like a brick shithouse**, it likely sparked few genuinely romantic encounters.

Ankle—As a verb, it's a synonym for *walk.* "C'mon, let's **ankle** over to the candy store." As a noun, it's a synonym for *woman.* As either part of speech, it's a 1930s–1940s example of metonymy, the rhetorical device by which a part of something is made to represent the whole thing. **Ankle** is a part of the act of walking and also part of a woman's anatomy—and in an age of fairly long skirts, an erotically charged part at that. Of course, so was the **skirt** itself. "Biff, what say we **ankle** over to dem **ankles** over there and see if we can't get lucky, huh?"

Angel—A word with multiple and diverse meanings during the 1920s–1930s, including
- a beautiful young woman (see also **flesh and blood angel**)
- a contributor to a theatrical (typically Broadway) production or to a political campaign
- a gay man (synonym for *fairy*)
- the victim (*mark*) of a confidence game.
  Note that the first two meanings are still current.

Bank's closed—I don't want to kiss or make out right now. This was said by a Roaring Twenties girl who didn't feel like roaring, at least not at the moment. "Look, Joe, you're a nice guy, but the **bank's closed**."

Biscuit—A **flapper** known to be amenable to petting. The origin of the expression is unknown.

Built like a brick shithouse—Said of a curvaceous, sexually attractive woman. The phrase was common in southern Canada and throughout the United States from the early twentieth century through the 1950s and is still occasionally heard, almost exclusively from the mouths of men past fifty. Its origin dates from a time and rural place in which a *brick* outhouse was a remarkable rarity indeed, the vast majority being ramshackle affairs cobbled together of wood. Thus, to be **built like a brick shithouse** is not only to be solidly female, but also to be first-rate, even luxurious. In the South, during the 1930s, the phrase was often embellished: "**Built like a brick shithouse** *with hot and cold folding doors and running water*." Curiously, in the UK, the phrase is sometimes applied to a well-built man, especially an athlete or sports figure.

Cash or check?—Do we kiss now or later? The response might be **Cash, please** (kiss me now) or **Check** (later). The catchphrase, encountered mostly in popular literature from the 1930s and 1940s, is not as mercenary as it may seem, since the word *cash* does at least sound like *kiss*.

Chassis—A woman's body, especially an attractive one. By the 1930s, guys were crazy about cars, and it must have seemed natural to apply an automotive term to another male object of desire. But why **chassis** instead of, more simply, *body*? The **chassis** is the *frame* on which the body is built, and *frame* is another word for the human body when considered from the point of view of *build*. The word also allowed the rhyming combination **classy chassis**, as in "That dame's got one **classy chassis**."

Chippy or **chippie**—A woman of easy virtue; a party girl. Strictly speaking, a **chippy** is not a prostitute, although she does allow men to pick her up in bars, treat her to drinks and dinner and possibly other gifts short of cash payment for sex. Although closely identified with tough-guy patois, the term dates to the mid-nineteenth century and is still in use today. Many people assume that it is a variation on *cheapie*, implying a cheap woman, a woman whose virtue is cheaply bought; more likely, however, the word derives from the *chipping sparrow* (familiarly called a **chip** or **chippie**), the commonest form of sparrow found in American cities. The **chippy** is therefore the most common of American "birds."

Daddy—A male lover, typically an older man who supports his younger girlfriend financially; a sugar daddy. The origin of the term is African American, from the 1910s or earlier. By the 1920s, its use spread to the white community, where a **daddy** was usually the older companion of a (much) younger **flapper**.

Dish—A really good-looking, eminently desirable woman. This was especially popular during the perpetually hungry Great Depression, when comparison to a delicious meal was genuinely desirable rather than blatantly offensive. The term is still used somewhat tongue-in-cheek. By the 1960s, women began using it to refer to particularly attractive men.

Dreamboat—A sexually attractive man or woman. The term was sufficiently novel to merit enclosure in quotation marks in a story about **"dreamboat"** British actor James Mason in an Associated Press wire story from the 1940s. The origin of the term is not known, but it may be significant that, also dating from the late 1930s and early 1940s, **dreamboat** was used to describe any beautiful, luxurious, and highly desirable automobile.

Drugstore cowboy—A loafer who hangs out in drugstores and tries to pick up girls at the soda fountain. This was the meaning of the phrase in the 1940s and 1950s. In some Western communities, both during and after this era, a **drugstore cowboy** was a young man who posed as a cowboy even though he had never actually punched cattle for a living. Beginning from the early 1960s on, **drugstore cowboy** has mainly referred to an addict who abuses illegally obtained prescription (as opposed to street) drugs.

Flapper—A worldly young woman of the 1920s, with the implication of casual allure and casual promiscuity. Perhaps the most iconic word of the Roaring Twenties, **flapper** is nevertheless something of an etymological mystery. It is certain that the word, though associated with Prohibition-era America, was in use far earlier. An instance of **flapper** meaning *prostitute* was recorded in England in 1631, and by the nineteenth century, Londoners were using it to describe an underage prostitute as well as any adolescent girl perceived as overly "forward" or possibly oversexed. The word also seems to have been applied freely to any adolescent female or young woman. Some etymologists believe this came from a comparison to a young bird ("chick") flapping about as it learns to fly; others think it a reference to the traditional adolescent hairdo, a plaited pigtail that *flaps* against the girl's back.

Flapper appeared with some regularity in British newspapers and magazines by the beginning of the twentieth century and was defined in 1908 by *The Times* of London as "a young lady who has not yet been promoted to long frocks and the wearing of her hair 'up.'" Whatever else this definition may signify, it indicates that, by this time, the equation between **flapper** and *prostitute* was no longer active. In the decade before the 1920s, the **flapper** was a familiar character type in popular plays staged in London and New York. At that time, the word was generally understood to mean a flirtatious young woman, although some described the type more precisely as a girl who "has just come out."

By the era of World War I, when young women were inducted into the workforce to take the place of the men who had marched off to battle, **flapper** became an increasingly common term on both sides of the Atlantic to describe a generation of young women whose experience of the world had liberated them socially and sexually. It was this sense that developed most fully in the 1920s. All of this said, however, many authorities believe that the **flapper** label of the Roaring Twenties had less to do with a long etymological pedigree than with current appearance. The jerky, frenetic, almost mechanical movements of the popular dances of the era made "flappers" of everyone. It has even been asserted that the wide-cuffed (and therefore "flapping") Russian boots some young women wore as a convenient place to hide a gin or whiskey flask was the immediate source of the term. See **bootleg**.

Although a **flapper** may be a party girl, a guy might still have to deal with her dad, who was known as a **dapper**.

Flesh and blood angel—An extremely beautiful woman. Reported from the 1920s, but compare "Earth Angel (Will You Be Mine)," a doo-wop hit by The Penguins in 1954. See also **angel**.

Gams—A woman's legs. A tough guy never calls a woman's legs *legs*. Acceptable terms include **drumsticks, pins, pillars, stems, uprights, getaway sticks**, and **gams**. Although **gams** was made popular by the **hard-boiled** detective fiction of the 1930s and 1940s, the word goes back to the eighteenth century, when it was shady, even criminal, slang for *legs*—either male or female. It may have come from the Italian *gamba* (leg) or from the English word *gamb*, a heraldic term denoting the representation of a leg on a coat of arms. This word may itself come from the Italian *gamba* or the French *gambe*.

Get a wiggle on—Get a move on (addressed to a woman). An impudent expression from the Roaring Twenties, **get a wiggle on** makes pointed reference to the movements of a curvaceous young lady in the close-fitting sheaths of the **flapper** era.

Glad rags—Party or evening clothes. Used in the 1920s through the 1930s for both men's and women's fanciest duds.

Jelly roll (or **Jelly-roll**)—Vagina; the sex act; a consummate (and consummating!) lady's man. In all of these senses, the word entered the language via African American speech by the mid- to late 1800s. It became especially popular among African American musicians, especially early jazz musicians, and is the moniker by which the world came to know the great ragtime pianist, band leader, and composer born in New Orleans as Ferdinand Joseph LaMothe (1885–1941): Jelly Roll Morton. He acquired the name when, at age fourteen, he was hired to play piano in a "sporting house" located in the New Orleans red light district known as Storyville.

Long drink of water—A tall, slender person. This formulaic phrase was so familiar to the generation of the 1930s and 1940s that its origin defies discovery. Usually applied to a young man rather than woman, its connotation is generally positive—the image of a tall, cooling drink implying satisfaction. Variations include **tall drink of water** and **tall glass of water**.

The phrase and its variations may be compared to other formulaic descriptions of tall men, including **tall, dark, and handsome**, which appeared in print as early as the 1910s. On the surface, this seems even more complimentary than **long drink of water**, but at least one prominent student of slang, the late Eric Partridge, believes it is actually a slight, since the phrase mimics a character-type description usually featured in the cheesy melodramas of the era. **Tall, dark, and handsome** spawned the negative-image phrase, which was noted in the 1970s: **fat, fair, and forty**. Also compare the formula, **strong, silent type**.

Make whoopee—Make out, make love, have sex. In the mid-nineteenth century, the phrase meant to have a noisy good time. By the 1910s and into the 1920s, the notion of a noisy good time was applied narrowly to making out or having sex. By the 1930s, the expression was used mainly by those old enough to remember what it had been like to **make whoopee** but who had long since lost the ambition or the ability to make it any more.

Nervous in the service—Applied to a man who is concerned about his ability to perform sexually—as in to "service" a woman. Of World War II vintage, this jingle-rhyming double entendre ostensibly described a draftee who was anxious about his stint in the army (was **"nervous in the service"**), but it was really all about worry over an impending sexual encounter. "**Nervous**

in the service? Don't drink too much, or you'll get the **whiskey dick** for sure."

Oomph girl—A sexually attractive woman; a **dish**. The phrase was coined by the Warner Bros. publicity department in 1939 to promote film star Ann Sheridan (1915–1967). The red-haired beauty was popular with **GI**s as a pinup girl during World War II and reigned during this era as the studio's number one sex bomb. The **oomph girl** phrase was widely applied to any **tomato**. See **sweater girl**.

Skirt—A woman, especially an available woman (or woman thus perceived). Some authorities (such as Robert L. Chapman in *The Dictionary of American Slang*) see the origin of this term in the nineteenth century, whereas others (including Tony Thorne, *Dictionary of Contemporary Slang*) trace it back to the sixteenth century. The second guess, for an older origin, seems the more plausible because *skirt* (in the sense of a woman's characteristic garment) dates from at least the fourteenth century, and the linguistic process of metonymy is a very common feature of language creation. In metonymy, an object closely associated with another object is made to stand for that second object. For example, we speak of the White House when our meaning is a reference to the president and his administration, or of the Crown in referring to the British government. Similarly, **skirt** is a metonym for a woman. Despite its likely venerable origin, **skirt** (as a synonym for woman) became highly popular during the late 1930s and through the period of World War II and well into the 1950s. Occasionally heard as well is **pro-skirt**, a synonym for *prostitute* (a "professional skirt").

In movies, **skirt** is often pronounced with an exaggerated Brooklyn accent to suggest its extreme colloquial nature: **skoit**. "That guy goes after any **skirt** that comes his way." (That is, he's a **skirt chaser**.)

Struggle buggy—The backseat of a car as a venue for **making whoopee**. The notion of *struggle* may reflect early-twentieth-century notions of female modesty or the perceived obligation of a "good girl" to resist relinquishing her virtue. On the other hand, it may simply reflect the cramped quarters of an automotive backseat—especially the rumble seat, the small exterior seat of some 1920s–1930s coupes, which folded out on hinges from where the trunk is on a more modern car.

Sweater girl—A well-endowed young woman. The phrase was used specifically to describe certain voluptuously proportioned actresses of the 1940s and 1950s (most notably Jane Russell and Lana Turner), who emphasized their bustline by wearing tight sweaters. **Sweater girl** was soon applied to any young woman who adopted the tight-sweater fashion to enhance her figure. The phrase was also adopted by the fashion industry itself to describe sweaters as well as bras designed to accentuate the positive.

Takes two to tango, it—It can't happen without the consent (or connivance) of two parties. The sentence is often applied to romance, especially illicit romance; that is, the proposition that so-called seduction requires a seducer as well as a willing seducee. The saying also applies more generally to any situation that requires cooperation, collaboration, conspiracy, or connivance. Although most authorities believe it originated in the popular song "Takes Two to Tango," published in 1952 by Al Hoffman and Dick Manning and turned into a hit by Pearl Bailey that year, the phrase has been reported as current in the 1930s, which suggests that the song lyric was taken from what was already a popular saying and, in turn, made the saying even more popular.

That's all she wrote—That's the end of it, with the implication of a bitter end. The expression is used to indicate any ending, especially an abrupt or unpleasant one: "Look, babe, I'd like to take you to dinner, but we used up all my cash at lunch. **That's all she wrote**." The origin of the catchphrase is romantic—a reference to the World War II GI fighting in Europe or the Pacific who answers mail call one day only to receive a "Dear John" letter from his erstwhile sweetheart: "Well, she broke it off with me. **That's all she wrote**." (Or possibly, "Well, she broke it off with me. **'That's all,' she wrote**.")

More recently, beginning in the 1960s, the catchphrase has been used to express satisfaction after a particularly productive trip to the bathroom: "Ah! **That's all she wrote**."

Tomato—A woman perceived as ripe, luscious, and ready to be plucked. The word was probably in use to describe a desirable female as early as 1900, but it rose to prominence during the 1920s and remained current well into the 1950s. It survives today as an expression of politically incorrect humor.

Torcher—A (female) singer of **torch songs**. **Torch song**, which describes a genre of popular sentimental music in which a female (usually) singer bemoans love lost either through betrayal or the non-responsiveness of her would-be lover, was first used about 1930. The singer "carries a torch" (harbors an intense passion) for the object of her song. The genre became so popular through the 1950s that the term **torch singer** was somewhat ironically abbreviated to **torcher**, with the pun on *torture* both obvious and intended.

Vamp—An alluring, seductive, sexually aggressive woman. The word is a shortened form of *vampire* and therefore suggests the predatory nature of the **vamp**'s sexuality. The word was born with the sensational 1915 film *A Fool There Was*, in which the sexy silent-screen star Theda Bara (1885–1955) played the Vampire, a serial seductress notorious for living off the men she ensnares, bleeding them white, and leaving them ruined. The movie's story and theme were inspired by Rudyard Kipling's 1897 poem "The Vampire," which, in turn, had been inspired by a Philip Burne Jones painting depicting a raven-haired woman atop a prostrate man whom she has apparently drained of life. "A fool there was," the poem begins, "and he made his prayer / . . . To a rag and a bone and a hank of hair / (We called her the woman who did not care), / But the fool he called her his lady fair . . . ."

Wash my hair tonight, **I have to** (or **tomorrow**, **next Thursday**, etc.)—A pointedly lame excuse for turning down an invitation; a brush-off. Hard to pin down when this classic was born, but it dates from an era when hair washing was a ritual for a woman, done every week or two, not every day. Throughout the era from the

1920s through the early 1960s, a woman's hairstyle typically required an elaborate setting that was meant to last a while. So back in the day, the excuse was not quite as hollow as it sounds now; nevertheless, it sent an unmistakable message of rejection.

Whiskey dick—Alcohol-induced impotence.

MACDUFF: What three things does drink especially provoke?

PORTER: Marry, sir, nose-painting, sleep and urine. Lechery, sir, it provokes, and unprovokes; it provokes the desire, but it takes away the performance; therefore, much drink may be said to be an equivocator with lechery: it makes him, and it mars him; it sets him on, and it takes him off; it persuades him, and disheartens him; makes him stand to, and not stand to; in conclusion, equivocates him in a sleep, and, giving him the lie, leaves him.

—William Skakespeare, *Macbeth*, act II, scene III

Your barn door is open—Your fly's unzipped. The expression came into use at a time—probably in the 1930s—when most Americans still lived on farms or close to farming communities. More sophisticated urbanites of the era might instead have warned, **Hey, mister, your fiddle case is open**.

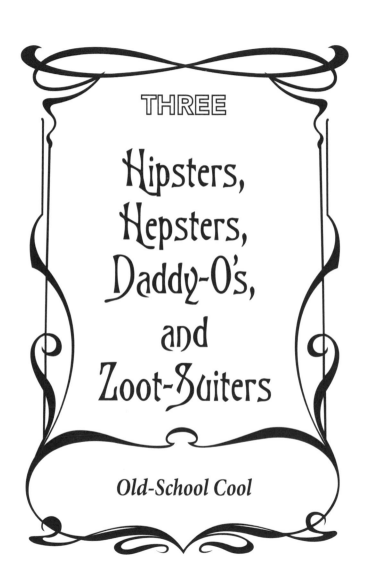

THREE

Hipsters, Hepsters, Daddy-O's, and Zoot-Suiters

Old-School Cool

lligator—A sharp, flashy, unbearably **hip**, overwhelming masculine man; by the 1930s, more narrowly applied in African American **jive** talk to any 100-percent committed fan of swing music and swing/**jive** culture; even more narrowly used by *black* jazz musicians to describe *white* jazz musicians or *white* devotees of the music.

The life of the word was extended into virtual immortality by the formulaic greeting and response "See you later, alligator"/ "In a while, crocodile." Although this Q & A catchphrase was in vogue by the mid-1930s, it was elevated to the status of verbal icon years later, in 1956, by white rock 'n' roll pioneer Bill Haley's hit song "See You Later, Alligator." The song—and phrase—was so pervasive that **hipsters** in Singapore, which was torn by political upheaval in the mid-1950s, took to greeting each other with, "See you later, agitator" and responding, "When it's quieter, rioter."

Ultimately bounded neither by geography nor race, the lineage of **alligator** stretches back to the mid-nineteenth century, when the word was British Cockney rhyming slang for *later.* If a denizen of London's Spitalfields, Stepney, Wapping, Bow, or Mile End needed an alternative to an uppity *ta-ta,* he'd depart with a friendly "See you **alligator**," meaning "See you later."

All reet!—All right. Pure 1930s African American **jive** talk, variations of which include "All reat!" and "All root!" The exclamation doubtless owes its survival (outside of a few slang dictionaries) to "Are You All Reet?," a song Cab Calloway wrote with Allan Clark and Jack Palmer, recording it with his orchestra on January 16, 1941. It asks the burning question, "All I want to know, / are you all reet?," and answers it too: "Yes, we're all reet!"

Ain't comin' on that tab—I don't agree to (or with) that. This vivid specimen of African American **jive** talk originated in Harlem during the 1930s and spread beyond Upper Manhattan to the rest of the country via popular music and the entertainment industry before dying out by about 1950. The literal sense of the expression is "Don't include me on that bar bill [tab]" or "Don't count on me to share that expense." It is found in *The New Cab Calloway's Hepster's Dictionary* (1944), the author observing that this expression was often abbreviated to "**I ain't comin'**." To the uninitiated, this must have sounded quite ordinary; those in the know, however, mentally completed the sentence to produce the original, colorful figure of speech.

Armstrongs—Virtuoso trumpet licks played in the highest register of the instrument. The term was used beginning in the 1930s and refers, of course, to the first great soloist in jazz, cornetist, trumpeter, and singer Louis "Satchmo" Armstrong (1901–1971).

Baked wind—Hot air; that is, empty talk. Among **hipsters**, originality was held in high esteem; therefore, common phrases were frequently translated into less common and always witty variations.

Barbecue—A girlfriend; a beautiful girl; more vulgarly, a tasty piece. Heard among African American musicians, the word figured in the title of Louis Armstrong's 1927 hit song "Struttin' with Some Barbecue."

Beat—The name and concept at the core of the Beat Generation of the 1950s. Jack Kerouac (1922–1969), the quintessential novelist (*On the Road*, 1957) of the Beat Generation, is given credit for popularizing the phrase in 1948 as a label for an emerging postwar anti-establishment cultural, artistic, and political movement among young people, mainly in New York City. The **beat** part of the name did not originate with Kerouac, however, but with another Beat Generation writer, John Clellon Holmes (1926–1988), whose *Go*, predating *On the Road* by five years, is generally considered the first novel of the **Beat** movement. More precisely, the term seems to have emerged from a conversation between Holmes and Kerouac, in which Holmes contended that **beat** expressed a world-weariness in the sense of being beaten down by false and alien social, spiritual, and cultural values. Kerouac immediately seized on the word, acknowledged Holmes's definition of it, but insisted on expanding the meaning to include the connotation of *up***beat** and the spiritual term ***beat***ific. Both men agreed that bebop jazz was very much a part of being **beat**, and so the musical dimension of the term was always important. See **beatnik**.

Beatnik—A word coined to describe members of the **Beat** Generation; the late 1950s incarnation of the **hipster**. The concept of being **beat** was defined and disseminated by Jack Kerouac and other writers of what Kerouac called the Beat Generation. In the mainstream media, those who espoused **Beat** Generation values were often subject to ridicule and stereotyping, and in an article published in the *San Francisco Chronicle* on April 2, 1958, Pulitzer Prize–winning columnist Herb Caen (1916–1997) coined **beatnik** to describe followers of Kerouac, poet Allen Ginsberg, and others associated with the **Beat** Generation. The work combined **beat** with the suffix of *Sputnik*, the Soviet satellite orbited the year before. Ginsberg and others objected to the word as demeaning a sincere and serious literary, cultural, spiritual, and political movement founded on important anti-establishment values. **Beatnik**, however, came to be associated with an image of loafing pseudo-intellectuals, dressed in black, sporting berets and goatees (men) or jeans and Jean Seberg sweaters (women), reciting indecipherable poetry, and living (on someone else's dime) in New York's Greenwich Village, where they consumed bebop and folk music in smoky clubs.

Beat to my socks—Totally broke. Current among African American jazz musicians by the 1930s.

Beef—To say or declare. "Did *he* **beef** that **jive** to you?" For a different kind of **beef**, see chapter 1, "Gumshoes, Gunsels, Mugs, and Molls."

Boo—As an adjective, excellent; as a noun, marijuana. These days, **boo** is most familiar as an African American synonym for *sweetheart, sweetie, darling,* and the like. During the late 1940s and early 1950s transition from the reign of the **hipster** to the era of the **beatnik**, however, **boo** was used by whites as well as blacks as an alternative to *excellent* or *fine*: "Charlie Parker blows a **boo** sax." Its meaning could be intensified by adding the adverb *deadly*: "Charlie Parker blows a **deadly boo** sax." Such **deadly boo** experiences could be intensified, of course, by indulging in a little **boo**: weed. As a synonym for *marijuana*, **boo** may have been derived from *jabooby,* a now-obsolete African American term for marijuana. That word is still sometimes heard in African American communities in the sense of a long, rambling, and ultimately unenlightening explanation or, more to the point, bullshit.

Boot—Give me (something), or pass (something to) me. The implication is that fulfilling the request takes little effort: Don't trouble yourself to *hand* it to me, just *kick* it over. See also **Knock me a kiss**.

Bust your conk—Do your utmost; work your hardest. This is the African American **hipster**'s version of the white guy's "break your neck." *Conk* is the caustic (lye-based) chemical mixture applied to straighten kinky hair; it is also a term used to describe the resulting straightened hairdo. More generally, *conk* may be used to mean the *head* itself. Essentially, therefore, to **bust your conk** is to break you head in order to get something done.

Cat—Originally, as defined in *The New Cab Calloway's Hepster's Dictionary* (1944), any member of a swing band; the meaning broadened throughout the **beat** and **beatnik** eras to become simply a synonym for *man*, albeit with the connotation of a man who is cool, with it, or hip.

Chime—the time, the hour. This is the **hipster**'s version of the sailor's *bells*. Five o'clock is five **chimes**. It appeared in *The New Cab Calloway's Hepster's Dictionary*.

Comes on like gangbusters—A sensational showing or performance. According to *The New Cab Calloway's Hepster's Dictionary* this still-popular phrase originated among hip jazz musicians, who used it to describe any all-out sensational musical or dance performance. The origin of the plural noun was doubtless *Gang Busters*, an extremely popular radio police drama that ran from 1935 (initially as *G-Men*) through 1957 and always began with a strident succession of police whistles, tires squealing, machine guns rattling, sirens wailing, and convicts marching. This arresting (so to speak) cacophony is what it meant to **come on like Gang Busters**. An odd variant was **comes on like a test pilot**, and as the original phrase wore thin, it was often abbreviated to **comes on**, as in "That **cat** really **comes on**, don't he?"

Copacetic (everything's, with me)—Everything's just fine and dandy. **Copacetic** made its dictionary debut in *Webster's Second International,* 1934, classified as slang, the entry making no guess at the word's origin. In 1979, nearly half a century after the height of the word's popularity, a Professor Joseph T. Shipley informed slang maven Eric Partridge that the scholarly consensus was for a Yiddish origin or, more precisely, Hebrew via Yiddish: *kol b' ts dik,* meaning "everything is in justice" (that is, *all is well*). A few scholars, however, believe the word originated in African American slang, specifically emanating from Harlem during the cultural ferment of the Harlem Renaissance in the 1910s and '20s. A leading chronicler of the Harlem Renaissance, Carl Van Vechten, defined *kopastee* in 1926 as "an approbatory epithet somewhat stronger than *all right.*"

While **copacetic** is now obsolete, its appeal endures, and it is still used from time to time for its pleasing retro effect.

Q: "How're you doing?"

A: "Oh, everything's **copacetic.**"

Creeps out like *The Shadow* —A musical effect, performance, or performer that makes a big impression (see **comes on like gangbusters**) but does so in a very subtle, sophisticated, super-suave manner. As the origin of **comes on like gangbusters** can be traced to the *Gang Busters* radio program, so **creeps out like *The Shadow*** is a reference to *The Shadow*, a very popular radio serial from the 1930s based on stories published earlier in pulp magazines. The title character was a combination super sleuth and vigilante who possessed powerful psychic crime-fighting powers. He was a suave and mysterious figure, sometimes voiced by none other than Orson Welles, who signed on ("creeped out") with a deep-voiced and sinister "Who knows what evil lurks in the hearts of men? The Shadow knows!"

Crumb crushers—Teeth. Reported by **hipster** Cab Calloway in 1944.

Dicty—High-class, smart (in the 1920s sense of stylish and sophisticated). African American **hipster**

talk from the 1920s. The online *Urban Dictionary* reports the word in the dialogue of a 1927 "race" movie (a film made by a black movie company for black audiences) in which the heroine is courted with, "Leave that **dicty** man and come with me."

Do me a solid—Request for a favor. "Man, you gotta **do me a solid**. I need you to cosign a loan." See **solid**.

Drape—Suit of clothes. The word may derive from either *drapery* (curtain) or *drape*, the tailor's term for how a suit jacket hangs off a man's shoulders and pants hang from the waist.

Frisking the whiskers—Warming up for a jam session. Remember, swing musicians are **cats**, and like cats, they preen before they pounce.

Frolic pad—Nightclub. An example is the famous Frolic Room on Hollywood Boulevard, which opened its doors in the 1930s—a fact that suggests that decade as the origin of **frolic pad**.

Gabriels—Trumpet players, especially those in a big band. The angel Gabriel appears in the Old Testament as well as the Koran as a messenger from God. Christians picture him as an angel who blows a trumpet to signal the End of Days and the general resurrection at the Last Judgment. Although this tradition is not rooted in the Bible itself, it has proven enduring.

Got your boots on! and **Got your glasses on!**—The first exclamation means that you're with it, a **hipster**, and you are wise. The second means that you are stuck up, snooty, and a **high hat**. Both are specimens of "original" Harlem **jive** as published in *The New Cab Calloway's Hepster's Dictionary*.

Hepster—Someone who is **hep** to the **jive**; that is, someone up-to-date; often more specifically, a knowledgeable fan of jazz and hot swing. In urban African American communities such as Harlem, **hepster** dates from before the 1920s, and by the 1930s was being displaced in those communities by **hipster**. Some authorities believe that **hep** (and therefore **hepster**) derives from the army drill sergeant's cadence call, *Hep, hep, hep, two, three, four.* You were either in step or out of step: **hep** or not **hep**. A variant on **hepster** is **hepcat**, which somewhat more narrowly implies being an aficionado of hot jazz.

High hat—As a verb, to snub someone out of a false sense of social superiority; as a noun, a person who **high hats** others. The phrase was current in the 1920s and seems to have originated among jazz musicians, who later used the phrase to describe a set of two cymbals, one on top of the other, operated by a foot pedal. The original expression alludes to the tall silk hat that tops off snooty white-tie evening or opera dress. See **igg**.

Hipster—A later (mid-1930s through the 1950s) version of **hepster**. The newer term has a broader cultural connotation than **hepster**. Whereas the earlier term was centered on an appreciation of jazz and hot swing, the later term includes a musical dimension but also implies a more all-encompassing coolness and knowingness (being **hip**). While **hepster** has faded into quaint antiquity, **hip** continues to be used as an adjective for *contemporary, with-it, trendy,* or *fashionable.*

Icky—A dense person, a **square**, the anti-hipster. One of the most common hipster terms of the 1930s, the word could also be used to mean overly sentimental, maudlin, corny; in short, patently uncool. The word is, of course, still in general use as a descriptive adjective, meaning *repulsive, revolting, distasteful,* or, physically, *gooey, sticky,* or *viscid*; however, these meanings seem to have developed in the early 1930s from the **jive-hipster** label for a **square**.

Igg—Ignore. This is a more direct snub than the **high hat**. "Hey, who are *you* to **igg** *me*, man?"

Jack—What you call any male friend. This was universal among African American jazz musicians in the 1930s and 1940s; however, its use as a generic name for a man was recorded in the UK as far back as 1706. For alternative meanings, check out **jack** in chapter 1, "Gumshoes, Gunsels, Mugs, and Molls." See also **pops**, below.

Jelly—Anything gratis; on the house. A Harlem club owner who really dug a musician's set might invite him over: "Have a drink, **Pops**. It's **jelly**." Compare to **jelly roll** in chapter 2, "Daddies, Dishes, Dreamboats, and Drugstore Cowboys."

Jive—A word with many meanings, including the hip street speech of Harlem from the 1920s through the

1940s; swing music of the 1930s and 1940 as played by African American musicians—that is, fast and hard-driving; high-velocity swing dancing, generally as performed by African Americans; and marijuana. On the negative side, **jive** might mean to deceive ("Don't **jive** me, man") or might be applied to nonsense or worthless talk ("Don't give me that **jive**, man.") or to cheap, fake, or worthless merchandise ("That **jive short** of yours is gonna break down before you drive it round the block").

Joint is jumpin', the—This party is hot! In 1937, pianist-composer Fats Waller wrote "The Joint Is Jumpin'," which defines the title phrase as "a new expression/ along ol' Harlem way" intended to describe a place where "everything is in full swing."

Knock me a kiss—Give me a kiss. The implication is casual rather than romantic. **Knock** could also be used in other phrases in place of *give*, as in "**Knock** me a reefer, **boo**." Also see **boot**.

Lay some iron—Tap dance. The phrase is from the 1930s, and the reference is to the metal taps on the heel and toe of a tap shoe. "That **cat** can really **lay some iron**!"

Lay your racket—Sell something, promote an idea, make a (business) proposition. "**Lay your racket** on me, man. What'll it cost me *this* time?" The phrase is African American **jive** talk from the 1930s, but **racket** itself was in mainstream use as a synonym for *trade, business*, or *profession*. The linkage to the traditional meaning of **racket**, an illegal business or operation, current in the UK by the mid-nineteenth century, was partly irony but mostly tough-guy cynicism.

Lily whites—Clean bedsheets (a luxury for many jazz musicians in the 1930s).

Line—Price. A 1930s–1940s **hipster** didn't ask what something cost, he asked for "the **line** on these

threads." If another **hipster** replied to the first **hipster's** query, he always doubled the price, so that the **line** on a $50 **zoot suit** came out as $100. See **tick**.

Main man—Best, most trusted friend. Often used as flattery to secure a favor: "You gotta help me out. You're my **main man**!"

Main on the hitch—The husband (often of a woman to whom one is attracted). "I'd dig her **knocking me a kiss**, but her **main on the hitch** looks like one mean **cat**."

Main squeeze—Best girl, favorite girlfriend. *Squeeze* puts the emphasis on the sex. Romantic **hipsters** called their steady girl their **main queen** instead.

Man in gray—The postman.

Mash me a deuce (fin, sawbuck, double saw-buck)—Lend me $2 ($5, $10, or $20). The implication of *mash* is to lay it in the palm of the hand, nice and firm. "**Mash me a fin**. I'm **melted out**."

Melted out—Flat broke.

Meter—**Jive** for a *quarter*. The name derives from the coin that would (in the 1930s and 1940s) buy you a half day's time on most municipal parking meters. An alternative is **ruff**, which likely derives from the milled (and therefore *rough*) edge of the quarter coin.

Mezz, the—The best, premium merchandise, the genuine article. Likely derives from the *mezzanine* in a theater auditorium, offering some of the best and most expensive seats in the house.

Moldy fig—Conservative enemies of bebop and modern jazz. The World War II era saw a revival of "traditional" swing jazz of the 1930s in opposition to the emerging modern jazz style later known as bebop. In 1942, jazz critic Bernard Gendron wrote an editorial in *Metronome* magazine titled "'Moldy Figs' and Modernists: Jazz at War" describing the conflict between musical conservatives and progressives. During the main phase of the bebop era (the immediate postwar years and into the 1950s), beboppers such as Dizzy Gillespie (1917–1993) resurrected **old figs** to refer to those who thought the older jazz was somehow purer and more legitimate than the new styles.

Mouse—Pocket. A pocket is sufficiently small, cozy, and dark to appeal to a rodent.

Neigho, pops (or **Jack**)—Nothing doing, mister; absolutely not. Combining *nay* with *high-ho*, this is an emphatic negative, a way of not just saying *No*, but *Hell, no*. The expression may be a nod to Cab Calloway and his trademark song "Hi-De-Ho," from 1947.

Ofay—Mildly derogatory term for any white person. Most modern linguists believe this African American word is of West African origin and is part of the heritage of slavery; however, there remains a widespread belief that it is nothing more than pig Latin for *foe*. A less popular etymology contends that **ofay** is a corruption of *au lait*, as in *café au lait*—coffee lightened with milk—and is an allusion to white skin.

Off the cob—Corny, old-fashioned, dated. Much **hipster** speech is built on indirection. Here, for example, instead of using the tired words *corny* or *cornball*, the speaker makes the leap to an object associated with corn (the cob) and an action (taking the corn off the cob). The result? A fresh expression built upon a tired cliché.

Orchestration—Overcoat. The term was used among African American musicians, especially those who played in big bands and swing bands. The idea is that a formally scored orchestration covers up the "body" of the music underneath. An alternative **jive** synonym for *overcoat* is **lead sheet**, a musical score that, unlike a full orchestration, specifies only the essential elements of a song: the melodic line, applicable chords (using symbols above the staff rather than notes), and lyrics.

Pad—bed. The **Beat** generation drew much of its language from **jive** and **hipster** talk, but when they appropriated **pad**, the **beats** and the **beatniks** expanded its 1930s–1940s meaning from *bed* to *room, apartment,* or *house*—any place you called home.

Pops—A form of address suitable for any man. **Pops** serves the same purpose as **Jack** and can be used regardless of the age of the person addressed.

Righteous—Magnificent, splendid, perfect, wonderful. "She is one **righteous** chick!" The word can also be used ironically, in the sense of *absolute, total,* or *complete,* as in: "That man is **righteous** trash."

Rock me—Send me, move me, impress me. The phrase was taken up by white rock 'n' roll performers and their audiences beginning in the late 1950s, but it originated among African American swing musicians at least two decades earlier.

Rug cutter—A very good dancer. **Cut a rug** was borrowed from the African American **hipster** community and widely used as a synonym for dancing through the 1950s, as in, "Want to **cut a rug**, baby?"

Sad—Of poor quality, shabby. The word puts the emphasis on the emotion of the person beholding the disappointing object or merchandise rather than on the object or merchandise itself.

Sadder than a map—Truly terrible. The origin of this strange expression defies easy analysis, but we can guess that the many lines on a map bring to mind the wrinkled visage of a sorrowful old man or old woman. The phrase may be used as a synonym for *really bad* or *just awful*. "That band last night was **sadder than a map**."

Sam got me (him, you)—I (he, you) was drafted. At least a quarter of the **hipster** era coincided with World War II, during which millions of young men were drafted. African Americans served in segregated units throughout the war. Draft notices were sent by mail (delivered by the **man in gray**) and began with this dreaded salutation, "Greetings from the President."

Set of seven brights—One week. In **jive**, a **bright** is a day, a **dim** an evening. **Seven brights**? A week, obviously.

Short—A car. This seems to have originated as African American slang in the 1920s and to have spread from there to the underworld, thence to the realm of the hot rod racing enthusiast.

Signify—To boast; also, to insult someone. Whites associated the term with African American musicians during the swing era—the 1930s through the 1940s— but it was used (and continues to be used) generally throughout the African American community.

Sky piece—One's hat. This is an example of pure **hipster** poetry.

Snatcher—A police officer; usually, a plainclothes detective. When this guy shows up, somebody is taken away.

Solid—As an adjective, wonderful, terrific, splendid. The word spread from the African American **hipster** community to the white mainstream by the 1950s, when it was often used in the campy phrase "**Solid, Jackson.**" As a noun, **solid** is a synonym for *favor*; see **do me a solid**.

Square—Originally, anyone who didn't dig jazz; the meaning soon broadened out to encompass any conventional, conservative person. Cab Calloway included the word in his *New Hepster's Dictionary* but it was current among African American jazz musicians as well as white swing musicians of the 1930s and may have been used in popular music circles during the preceding decade as well.

Take care of business—Execute with style and efficiency. This phrase appeared in the American black community early in the 1950s and remains current. It is often abbreviated **TCB**.

The Man—White authority, the white establishment; often more specifically, the law (police, judge, parole officer). By the 1960s, the phrase was adopted by young whites, minus the racial connotations, as a synonym for "the Establishment."

Threads—Clothing; one's outfit. The connotation is *stylish*. This word survived the **hipster** era, flourished among the **Beat** Generation, continued to be heard during the hippie years, and is still current today.

Tick—One minute. "I'll catch you in a few **ticks**." **Ticks** could also be used to express the hour of the day; however, as in replying to the question "What's the **line** on these **threads**?," the **jive** talker always doubled the actual hour. Thus *eight o'clock* was delivered as "**tick** sixteen.**" Presumably this **jive doubling** ritual was intended to separate **hipsters** (who were in the know) from **squares** (who were not).

Timber—A toothpick. Held between the teeth, its end practically chewed to sawdust, the toothpick was a key **hipster** accessory from the 1930s through the early 1950s. As with most accoutrements of the **jive** life, it was unthinkable to call it by its given name, and so the comic inflation **timber** must have come to seem just right.

Trilly—To leave, to depart. As far as can be determined, **trilly** is a kind of contraction of *really and truly*, as in the closing line of a letter: *Really and truly yours*; therefore, it is appropriate when leaving or signing off. "Time for me to **trilly**." More recently, **Trilly** (capital *T*) has been reported as a way of addressing a person perceived as "really and truly" dumb, as in "Beat it, **Trilly**." This meaning, however, did not apply in the **jive** or **hipster** era.

Truck—Used as a verb, it means to go somewhere. "Let's **truck** down to the Cotton Club." The etymology of the word seems obvious enough; to *truck* is to *transport* or *carry*, so the sense here is to *transport* or *carry* oneself somewhere. However, it is also true that Blind Boy Fuller (1907–1941) composed his blues classic "Truckin' My Blues Away" in 1937. In this song, the word **truckin'** is used to mean precisely what it rhymes with (that is, swap the *t* for an *f* and forget the *r*). Blind Boy encourages his "baby" to "keep on **truckin'**," day and night: "**Truckin'** my blues away." It may be that the double meaning of **trucking** (or **truckin'**) was already current among **hipsters** in 1933, when a style of dance called **Trucking** (or **Truckin'**) debuted at Harlem's legendary Cotton Club; however, the dance style is a kind of comic strut, possibly inspired by Willie Bryant's (1908–1964) imitation of a man walking along a New York City dockside, and was not seductive, let alone sexual. (Some authorities say the **Trucking** dance was actually already popular in late 1920s burlesque houses, and others believe it can even be traced all the way back to the minstrel shows that were performed by whites in blackface beginning in the 1830s.) It is most likely, therefore, that Blind Boy Fuller's prescription of **truckin'** as an earthy home remedy for the blues was original with the composer.

V-8—A girl who is too independent for a relationship, whether long- or short-term. The origin of the term is probably the eight-cylinder automobile engine, which is always ready to get up and go, and *not* the vegetable juice drink that was marketed as "Vege-min 8" in 1933 but really took off as a brand a few years later when the name was shortened to V-8 (acquired by the Campbell Soup in 1948).

Zoot suit—This caricature of a suit was the emblem of the American **hipster**, circa 1930 through the 1940s. The name is an example of what linguists call reduplication, with *zoot* reduplicating *suit*, and it aptly suggests the nature of the garment as a wild exaggeration of a conventional man's suit of clothes featuring an extravagant surplus of fabric. The word **zoot** itself was used among African American **hipsters** as a synonym for *wild* or *exaggerated.* A **zoot suit** coat had wide padded shoulders, enormous lapels, and a skirt length ending just above the knees, almost like an Edwardian frock coat. The trousers were very high-waisted, the ultra-wide legs sharply tapering to very tight cuffs pegged at the ankles. The style originated in Manhattan's Harlem among African Americans and Mexican Americans, then spread to Italians—all residents of that neighborhood during the 1930s. From these groups, the **zoot suit** became a fad among white **hipsters**. It was typically topped by a very broad-brimmed fedora adorned with a hatband of contrasting color.

For the ethnic groups among whom it originated, the **zoot suit** was an emblem of cultural pride and independence. In 1943, in Los Angeles, during World War II, a series of so-called **zoot suit** riots broke out between Anglo sailors and marines on the one hand and zoot-suited Latino youths. The servicemen professed outrage that the extravagant garments defied wartime rationing of fabric and were therefore blatantly unpatriotic. Within weeks of the L.A. riots, **zoot-suit** violence broke out between Anglos and Latinos in Chicago, Beaumont (Texas), San Diego, Evansville (Indiana), Detroit, Philadelphia, and New York City.

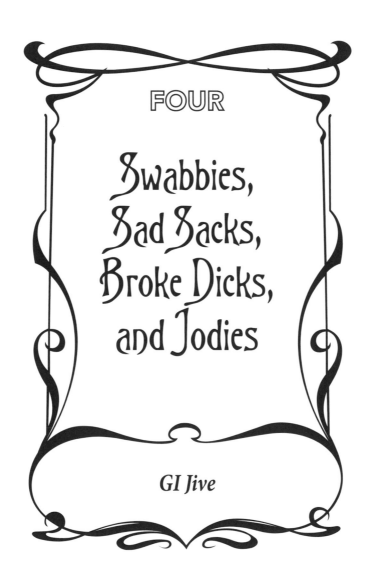

FOUR

Swabbies, Sad Sacks, Broke Dicks, and Jodies

GI Jive

rmy **strawberries**—Prunes. The practice of calling prunes **army strawberries** was a product of World War II and was motivated by two things. First: The U.S. Army made it a practice to paint everything olive drab (OD), so it was natural for soldiers to assume the army would not scruple to deface bright red strawberries, thereby transforming them into **army strawberries**: prunes. Second: Camp life, including changes in diet and sanitation problems, made diarrhea, and even dysentery, common complaints, as if one had been eating a diet of **army strawberries**—i.e., laxative prunes. "Man those **army strawberries** are giving me the **GI** trots."

Balls to the wall—All-out, maximum effort, or at full speed. Used by airmen of the U.S. Army Air Forces, this one's raunchy, but maybe not as raunchy as you think. The velocity of World War II–era propeller-driven aircraft was proportional to the revolutions per minute of the props, the speed of which was controlled by throttles, one per engine. In bombers and other two- to four-engine aircraft, the throttles were controlled by levers mounted in the center console between the pilot's and copilot's seats, one lever for each throttle and each lever topped by a ball-like grip. To obtain full speed, you pushed the throttles all the way forward, toward the firewall at the front of the cockpit. Full speed, therefore, required putting your **balls to the wall**. Metaphorically, the phrase was also used to describe any maximum effort: "Gentlemen, the general wants **balls to the wall** on this mission, **balls to the wall**."

Belly robber—An army cook or mess sergeant. Soldiers in both world wars sometimes marched to this song verse: "The biscuits in the army they say are mighty fine. / One rolled off the table and killed a pal of mine." See **SOS**.

Brain bucket—U.S. Army slang for *helmet* during World War II. Soldiers knew that their steel helmets would not stop a bullet, but at least it would keep their brains close to their head.

Brass, the—The upper ranks of the U.S. military. Popularized during World War II, this derogatory term for the senior officer corps derived from the profusion of brass buttons and brass medals on the uniforms of the highest ranks. Sometimes these officers were called **brass hats**, in reference to the large metallic eagle emblem on the front of an officer's cap.

Broke dick—A soldier (and, later, anyone, soldier or civilian) with a medical condition that hinders him from performing certain tasks; also applied to equipment that is not operational. The term emerged during World War II and was also popular during the Korean Conflict. It is still occasionally heard today, but mostly in the army and Marine Corps. During the post–World War II period, homecoming vets carried it into the civilian sector, where it was used to describe anyone with a disability, real or put-on. "He's a regular **broke dick** when it comes to doing anything like honest work."

Buck—The lowest position in any military hierarchy. A **buck** private is a recruit, a step below private first class; a **buck** sergeant is the lowest rank of sergeant, a step above corporal. Many authorities believe that **buck** in this sense is a reference to one dollar, the lowest denomination and, therefore, the least in the hierarchy of currency. It is also possible that the word's origin is to be found in **buck**, a male deer, the connotation being a *young* male.

Cigarette soup—Onion soup (and decidedly not the French gourmet variety). World War II veterans took this evocative term with them into civilian life. Onions were cheap and plentiful; thrown into boiling water, they made a soup that was a staple in army mess halls. Soldiers soon tired of it, coming to feel that it looked just like what you got if you filled a heavily used ashtray with water. "Ah, great! Another steaming bowl of **cigarette soup**."

Cunt cap—The soft, folding cap worn at times by members of all the service branches; in World War I and

World War II, it was often called an overseas cap, a crew cap, or a garrison cap. If a **GI** exercised his imagination, it was possible to see a resemblance between this cap and a vagina. Removed as they were from the companionship of the fairer sex, most **GIs** were inclined to exercise their imaginations vividly. **Cunt cap** was primarily used in the U.S. Army and U.S. Army Air Forces during World War II; sailors and marines generally referred to the folding crew cap as a **piss cutter**.

Crud—As an adjective, nonsense, bullshit; as a noun, a despicable person or an unpopular officer. Also, during World War I, a synonym for venereal disease. In civilian life as well as in the military, **crud** also meant dried semen. The general slang meaning of **crud** is any unspecified disease, typically with flulike or cold-like symptoms: "Not feeling well. I've got the **crud**." The word also describes dried food residue left, for example, on dishes or utensils, or other dried waste material. This sense explains the word's origin in the Middle English *curd*, which seems to have meant in the Middle Ages pretty much exactly what it means today.

Dogface—An enlisted man (non-officer, especially a private) in the infantry of the U.S. Army. The word came into use during World War II and survived into the postwar years. Originally derogatory, **dogface** became a kind of title of esteem to describe the unassuming, long-suffering, uncomplaining, battle-hardened victors in the "Good War." This positive image was developed by the likes of combat journalist Ernie Pyle (1900–1945) and combat cartoonist Bill Mauldin (1921–2003), both of whom celebrated, with unblinking gritty realism, the uncommon common American **GI**.

Doughboy—General term for a U.S. Army infantryman (non-officer) in the World War I era. The origin of this term is obscure and still hotly debated. What is certain is that although it is most closely associated with World War I, **doughboy** predates 1914–1918, and although the term was obsolete during World War II (1939–1945), some senior officers (most notably General Omar Nelson Bradley) persisted in using it. Many etymologists believe the word came about during the Civil War (1861–1865) and was a reference to the large buttons on army uniforms, which were thought to resemble doughboys—that is, bread dough that has been rolled thin and deep-fried. Other etymologists put the origin of the word about fifteen years earlier, to the era of the Mexican-American War (1846–1848). One explanation for that earlier origin is that after a long march through the dusty, dry terrain of Texas and Mexico, the soldiers were coated in whitish, powdery dust that made them look like unbaked dough. And so they were *dough boys*. Another suggestion is that the name came from the soldiers' practice of preparing field rations of mixtures of doughy flour and rice. Some historians believe that pipe clay, a white material used to clean and whiten the crossed garrison belts that were a part of the uniform of the Mexican War era, looked like raw dough. A few authorities, while conceding that **doughboy** might have come into being during the nineteenth century, insist that it emerged front and center during World War I because the soldiers of America's allies, Britain and France, thought that the stiff, high-collared olive drab uniforms worn by American soldiers made them look like gingerbread men— from which it was a very short step to **doughboys**.

GI (or **G.I.**)—As a noun, the generic name for any member of the U.S. armed forces, though typically applied to U.S. Army soldiers below officer rank; as an adjective, a modifier for anyone or anything in any way associated with the U.S. military or U.S. military life: "My **GI** shoes give me **GI** blisters." This initialism (as linguists call words that consist of initials) was most widely used in World War II (1939–1945), but it had emerged before World War I (1914–1918), dating at least as far back as 1907, when the initials **GI** were stamped into any piece of U.S. military equipment made of galvanized iron. Indeed, American **doughboys** in World War I often referred to incoming German artillery shells as "**GI**." By World War II, **GI** was universally understood to mean *government issue*—although some amateur etymologists have mistakenly insisted that the letters stand for *general infantry*. The "typical" soldier in World War II—the military "John Doe"—was known as **GI Joe**.

Gun—Penis (*never* to be confused with *rifle* or *sidearm*). Much military slang from the periods of major wars, when large numbers of men were inducted into the service, was intended to transform the recruit from a civilian into a soldier, to sever him from his former life, and to turn his affection from his girl to his rifle. One of the first things the green recruit had to learn was that a rifle is never to be referred to as a *gun*. Recruits who made

this mistake in World War II basic training were sometimes ordered to strip naked and repeat the following
chant, with appropriate hand gestures accompanying:

This is my rifle.
This is my gun.
This is for shooting.
This is for fun.

Gung-ho—Fanatically enthusiastic and committed; zealous. The word was universally popular in
the U.S. Marine Corps during World War II after it had
been introduced to the Corps by Major Evans Carlson
(1896–1947), who picked it up from New Zealander
Rewi Alley (1897–1987). Alley was a Western supporter
of the Communist Party of China and was one of the
founders of the party's Chinese Industrial Cooperative
Association. **Gung-ho**, Carlson explained in 1943, was
"the motto of the Chinese Cooperatives. . . . It means
Work Together—Work in Harmony." The major used
this concept in training the 2nd Marine Raider Battalion
(Carlson's Raiders). The 1943 movie *Gung Ho!*, about
the remarkable 1942 Raider Battalion assault on Makin
Island, introduced the term to American civilians. As
adopted into the cultural mainstream, however, **gung-**

ho lost its original meaning of "work together in harmony" and instead was used to describe any extremely enthusiastic, all-out, or hyper-zealous attitude, often with the connotation of near fanaticism. "The Cubs haven't won a World Series in 102 years, but Joe remains a **gung-ho** Cubs fan."

Jody—A mythical civilian who, remaining on the home front while others serve, lives a life of indulgence that included sleeping with the girls the soldiers left behind; the name for a military marching cadence featuring themes of homesickness and infidelity (also known as a **Jody call**).

Armies have been marching to call-and-response cadence chants at least since the days of the pre–Christian Roman legions. In the U.S. Army, however, during the World War II era, a specific kind of cadence developed around the mythical figure of **Jody** (also spelled **Jodie**), the stay-at-home civilian who (perhaps for medical reasons, real or fake) avoided the draft. Not only does **Jody** make time with the soldier's sweetheart (often called Susie in a **Jody call**), he sometimes takes advantage of the soldier's sister as well, enjoys home-cooked meals prepared by the soldier's mom, and even drives his car.

Jody calls survived World War II and are still very much a part of military life, mainly in U.S. Army basic training and U.S. Marine Corps boot camps. Untold thousands of **Jodies** have been composed, most of them crude, many of them obscene. For the 1949 World War II epic *Battleground*, Hollywood cleaned up a typical **Jody**. Note how the call and response refers to *left* and *right* as the soldiers march:

Drill sergeant: You had a good home but you left
Platoon: You're right
You had a good home but you left
You're right
Jody was there when you left
You're right
Your baby was there when you left
You're right
Sound off!
One, two
Sound off!
Three, four
Cadence count!
One, two, three, four—one, two . . . three, four!
They signed you up for the length of the war
I've never had it so good before
The best you'll get in a biv-ou-ac
Is a whiff of cologne from a passing WAC

Sound off!
One, two
Sound off!
Three, four
Cadence count!
One, two, three, four—one, two . . . three, four!
There ain't no use in going back
Jody's livin' it up in the shack
Jody's got somethin' you ain't got
It's been so long I almost forgot
Sound off!
One, two
Sound off!
Three, four
Cadence count!
One, two, three, four—one, two . . . three, four!
Your baby was lonely, as lonely could be
'Til Jody provided the company
Ain't it great to have a pal
Who works so hard just to keep up morale
Sound off!
One, two
Sound off!
Three, four
Cadence count!
One, two, three, four—one, two . . . three, four!

You ain't got nothin' to worry about
He'll keep her happy until I get out
An' you won't get home 'til the end of the war
In nineteen hundred and seventy four
Sound off!
One, two
Sound off!
Three, four
Cadence count!
One, two, three, four—one, two . . . three, four!

Jody calls have been intensively studied by folklorists, who believe that the name and character of "**Jody**" can be traced back to a figure from African American folklore known as Joe the Grinder, a guy always ready to take advantage of another man's absence.

Latrinegram—Any wild, unfounded rumor; in other words, a load of crap. Military life, especially during the chaos and uncertainty of World War II, was rife with rumor and gossip. Soldiers soon learned not to believe most of it, but nevertheless eagerly delivered every **latrinegram** that came their way. The word is, of course, a combination of *latrine* (the communal toilet facility in a barracks or camp) and the final syllable of *telegram.* "The latest **latrinegram** out of Headquarters Company is that we're shipping out in a week."

Million-dollar wound—A combat injury serious enough to merit being sent home but not serious enough to be life-threatening or permanently disabling or disfiguring. The phrase was popular during World War II. Many so-called **million-dollar wounds** (a shot through the foot, for example) were self-inflicted by soldiers suffering battle fatigue).

Mox nix—Makes no difference. Soldiers who served in the European Theater during World War II corrupted the German sentence *"Es macht nichts"* (it makes no difference) to these two phonetic syllables and carried the expression into the civilian realm after the war. It is likely that the utterance was inspired or at least influenced by **Moxie**, a popular soft drink of the period and itself an important word from the 1930s through the 1950s. (It should be noted that *nix*, which dates to the eighteenth century and is of British origin, was a common expression of negation through the mid-twentieth century, variously used as a synonym for *no, not,* and *nothing,* or to express a refusal or veto.)

Q: "Do you want to take in a movie this evening?"
A: "Mox nix."

Ninety-day wonder—Newly-commissioned second lieutenant graduate of the U.S. Army's Officer Candidate School (OCS) program. World War II caught the army with a critical shortage of company-grade officers: first and second lieutenants and captains. Neither the U.S. Military Academy (West Point) nor university ROTC programs could turn out enough officers to fill the needs of an explosively expanding army, so Major General Omar Bradley and others promoted a program to train selected enlisted men as officers in all of three months. Fairly or unfairly, these officer graduates were widely regarded as unqualified. The word *wonder* was intended as derogatory, an imitation of the puffery used to advertise a wide variety of "wonder" products. During World War II, the Korean War, and the early part of the Vietnam War (prior to 1970), OCS was derisively known as Oklahoma Cook's School. After World War II, **ninety-day wonder** was widely applied in the civilian world to any supervisor or manager subordinates disliked, thought incompetent, and believed had been promoted too quickly and without merit. See also **Sears Roebuck**.

Sears Roebuck—A brand-new second lieutenant. The demands of World War II combat resulted in the mass production of junior officers after just three months of training in Officer Candidate School (OCS; see **ninety-day wonder**). Such a green officer was sometimes referred to as a **Sears Roebuck**, after the name of the famous mail-order house. The idea was that the new officer had ordered his second lieutenant's bars (called a **butter bar** because of their gaudy gold plating) from the Sears Roebuck catalogue. Almost certainly, the *buck* syllable of *Roebuck* also suggested **buck**, army slang for the lowest step in the hierarchy of ranks.

Shit screen—A fall guy, scapegoat. This was the guy everyone automatically blamed for any foul-up in a squad or platoon. The term dates from World War II and is still in use. It was essential to have a reliable **shit screen** in order to avoid the effects of a **shit storm**, the misery the **brass** rained down upon the lower ranks whenever made unhappy.

SNAFU—Acronym for "situation normal: all fucked up"—though sometimes sanitized to "*fouled* up." The American military's love affair with official acronyms first blossomed during World War II, and it was not long before soldiers started coining some acronyms of their own, the most popular of which was **SNAFU**. The word, without its off-color connotation and, indeed, without a sense of its even being an acronym, came into general civilian speech even before the end of the war (that is, by the mid-1940s). A host of military variants on **SNAFU** never entered general civilian speech, however, and have mostly vanished even from colloquial military usage. These include **FTA**, fuck the army; **FUBAR**, fucked up beyond all recognition; **FUBB**, fucked up beyond belief; **FUBIS**, fuck you, buddy, I'm shipping (out)—meaning, "Don't bother me about that, it's your problem now"; **FUMTU**, fucked up more than usual; **GFU**, general fuckup; **JANFU**, joint army-navy fuckup, and **TARFU**, things are really fucked up.

SOS—Shit on a shingle; also, same old shit. In 1908, **SOS** was adopted as the international radiotelegraph Morse code signal for distress. At some time during World War II, those same initials were adopted in the enlisted men's mess as a signal of specifically gustatory distress. A staple of World War II military cuisine was creamed chipped beef on toast, unofficially and universally dubbed shit on a shingle: SOS. The utility of this acronym rapidly increased as the expression came to be more widely applied to signify any old lies, chores, or routines the army dished up day after day: Same Old Shit. In this latter sense, **SOS** entered, and has lingered in, general civilian speech, although it is sometimes sanitized to mean same old stuff or simply abridged and reduplicated to **same old same old**.

Submarine—A hospital bedpan. Why? Because it goes under you and is flooded periodically.

Swabbie—U.S. Navy sailor. The lowest-ranking sailors spent much of their time aboard ship *swabbing* (mopping) the deck. By the early twentieth century, therefore, they were universally known as **swabbies** or **swabs.** It was the navy equivalent of the infantry's **dogface.**

Tell it to the chaplain—I don't want to hear about your troubles. In theory, the role of the military chaplain is to see to the spiritual needs of the troops; in reality, the chaplain serves mainly as someone on whom to dump one's troubles, worries, complaints, and anxieties.

Washout—In the service, someone who failed to make it through an elite program, especially in the Air Corps; also used as a verb: "Straighten up and fly right! You don't want to **wash out** of flight school, do you? You don't want to be a **washout**." The word was in use in the U.S. Army Air service by the era of World War I. The term is one of those words that seem to have self-evident meaning, so no one has worked very hard to determine its origin. We do know that **washout** was a synonym for *crash landing* by the time of World War I. The word also describes structural failure due to flooding: "The swollen river created a **washout** that took the bridge with it." In the late nineteenth-century British army, practice targets were made of iron. The impact of a marksman's bullets was highlighted by a daub or *wash* of paint. Impacts that fell outside of the target zone were referred to as **wash-outs**. Whatever the origin, **washout** was a term of derision that could follow one long after he left the service. "You don't want anything to do with me. Don't you know I'm just a **washout**?"

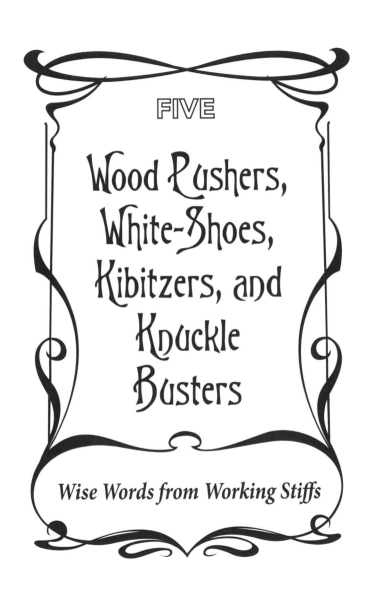

FIVE

Wood Pushers, White-Shoes, Kibitzers, and Knuckle Busters

Wise Words from Working Stiffs

in't we got fun!—A straightforward exclamation that later edged into sarcasm. If you're old enough to remember the 1921 Tin Pan Alley song of which this is the title (music by Richard A. Whiting and lyrics by Ray Egan and Gus Kahn), you're old enough to be dead. The original gist of the exclamation was expressed in the song's first chorus: "Not much money / Oh but honey / Ain't we got fun." The songwriters meant this as a straightforward expression of good times, but in the 1930s, it was used mainly as ironic sarcasm meaning, "We're screwed (as usual)."

You go outside. It starts raining soup.

"Ed!" you call to your dud of a husband inside. "It's raining soup! Quick, come out with something!"

He does, handing you a fork.

"**Ain't we got fun!**" you say.

Ameche—Telephone. Unless you are a classic film buff or just plain old, the equation of the odd-looking word **Ameche** with *telephone* will doubtless baffle you. In 1939, 20th Century Fox released *The Story of Alexander Graham Bell,* in which actor Don Ameche (1908–1993) shed both his customary persona as a dapper if slightly oily leading man / lady's man and his trademark manicured mustache to play the inventor. The movie's story line is as much about Ameche's courtship of Loretta Young (as the deaf Mabel Hubbard, whom the real Bell married) as it is about the invention of the telephone. As Bell's long-suffering assistant Thomas Watson ("Mr. Watson, come here. I want you"), Henry Fonda also plays against type, turning in a fine performance as a drily humorous sidekick. The movie was sufficiently popular to make **Ameche** a contender with **blower** and **horn** as a workingman's and tough-guy's alternative to *telephone*. "Hold the wire, Sam. My other **Ameche**'s ringing."

Another nail in my coffin—Yet something else that's gone wrong or gone against me. OK, so when Wall Street crashed in 1929, John Q. Investor took what was left of his money out of the stock market and put it in the bank. Then the bank went bust. "**Another nail in my coffin**," he said. The phrase was recorded as early as 1910 in Australia and eleven years later in England. Interestingly, according to Eric Partridge, long the preeminent scholar of English-language slang, the phrase may have originated as a response to being scolded for smoking cigarettes. In reply to a rebuke, the smoker lights up, takes a drag, exhales, and remarks, "**Another nail in my coffin**." *Coffin nail* (or just *nail*) was a synonym for *cigarette* long before the U.S. Surgeon General weighed in on the hazards of smoking.

Ball the jack—Work at top speed; make haste. Jim Burris and Chris Smith wrote a ragtime hit in 1913 titled "Ballin' the Jack," which provides instructions for some provocative dance-floor moves:

> *First you put your two knees close up tight,*
> *Then you sway 'em to the left, then you sway 'em*
> *   to the right,*
> *Step around the floor kind of nice and light,*
> *Then you twis' around and twis' around with all*
> *   your might.*
> *Stretch your lovin' arms straight out in space,*
> *Then do the Eagle Rock with style and grace.*
> *Swing your foot way 'round then bring it back,*
> *Now that's what I call "Ballin' the Jack."*

Some authorities believe that Burris (the lyricist) took the phrase from railroader's parlance for running a locomotive at top speed. In the nineteenth and early twentieth century, a railroad track signal did not consist of red, yellow, and green lights, but of a pole-mounted ball that was lowered to indicate a stop, raised halfway to indicate slow ahead, and lifted high to signal full speed. The latter signal was referred to as a *highball* and is the origin of the generic name of alcoholic mixed drinks served in tall glasses. A locomotive was referred to as a *jack*. Thus, to "(high)ball the jack" was to open the throttle of the locomotive to push it full speed ahead. By extension, **ball the jack** came to describe anything (but especially work) done at top speed.

While most students of folk language believe that the railroader's phrase preceded both the Burris lyric and the sense of working fast and was therefore the origin of both, some argue that *jack* as a synonym for locomotive was not recorded before the 1920s and therefore conclude that the song lyric came before *both* the railroad jargon *and* the more general sense of working fast—that, in fact, the popular lyric gave rise to both.

Barber—Talk, converse (both as noun and verb). A man may clam up to his wife, to the cops, or to a priest, but even the strong silent type opens up to his barber. By the 1930s, therefore, **barber** became a synonym for a conversation ("Let's sit down for a little **barber**") and for the act of conversing ("Let's you and me **barber** on that one, huh?").

Beezer—Nose; sometimes applied to the whole face. This is a word primarily from 1930s hobo culture, although it was also heard in the world of boxing: "The champ busted him one, right in the **beezer**." The origin of **beezer** is anyone's guess. It may be a variant of *schnozz* (from German via Yiddish *schnoz*), it may suggest a dog's (Bowser's) muzzle, or it may have been suggested by the example of **kisser**, for mouth.

Bindle stiff—Itinerant worker or other wanderer (such as a hobo) who carries his worldly possessions in a *bindle* (a piece of cloth tied into the form of a sack).

Born of the Depression, the term **bindle stiff** may refer to a hobo, but it is by no means synonymous with one; instead, it applies to any itinerant—migrant worker, criminal, or hobo—who ties up his belongings in a bindle. A variant, **bindle punk**, connotes an itinerant who is also a homosexual predator of boys and young men (also known as a *wolf*). See also **working stiff**.

Board stiff—A sandwich-board man. From the late nineteenth century well into the 1950s, the sandwich board (an advertisement consisting of two boards connected by straps and worn over the shoulders of a man, one board hanging over the chest, the other over the back) was a very popular form of urban publicity and advertising. The job of the **board stiff** was to walk with his sign up and down the streets. Hardly skilled labor, it barely paid a wage. See also **working stiff**.

Bump gums—Engage in a futile conversation. You can either **talk turkey**—have a productive conversation in which an understanding is reached or a deal made—or you can just **bump gums**: talk endlessly without useful result. "Look, I don't want to **bump gums**. Either pay or **take it on the arches**."

Butt me—Give me a cigarette. This imperative request was often followed by **Match me**, meaning, *Give me a light. Butt* is not only the mouth end of a used cigarette but is also a slang synonym for the cigarette itself—and one favored by tough guys and gals. Alternatives include **Cigarette me** and **Nail me—coffin nail** (or just **nail**) also being a working-class synonym for *cigarette*.

Buy you (or **me**) **a drink**—Pour you (or me) a drink. A phrase encountered in "smart" books and movies of the 1920s through the 1940s. A host of that era, in his home, might offer liquid hospitality with the phrase "Let me **buy you a drink**," or a guest in that home might make the request, "Why don't you **buy me a drink**?"

Cheap at half the price—A bargain. This odd expression, first recorded in the 1920s (but possibly of earlier vintage), is an example of what linguists call an "intense idiom," meaning that it really makes no sense because it says the opposite of what it means, namely, *This would be cheap even at double the price.* "Buddy, the car's got a few miles on it, sure, but for what *I'm* askin'? It would be **cheap at half the price**."

Chew—Dine. An invitation to get a bite to eat, circa 1935, might consist of just two words: "Let's **chew**."

Circus bees—Body lice. During the Great Depression, joblessness, homelessness, and general vagrancy were commonplace. People living in close quarters in shantytowns (see **Hooverville**) and in **flophouses** with minimal sanitation and only the clothes on their backs quickly learned to make their peace with vermin. One way was to make a grim joke of it all by comparing body lice to the carnival sideshow attraction known as the flea circus, in which fleas appear to perform such circus acts as kicking lightweight balls, pulling carts, and even playing musical instruments. Instead of *circus fleas*, the lice were dubbed **circus bees**.

Coffee-and-doughnut—Cheap, nearly valueless. The origin of this phrase is obscure, except that it was born in an era when a coffee and doughnut made for the very cheapest "meal" you could get. A variation is **coffee and cakes**, which similarly refers to something of negligible value. "The handle on this hammer broke right off. It's strictly **coffee-and-doughnut** merchandise."

Cold enough to freeze the balls off a brass monkey—Pretty darn cold. Etymologist Eric Partridge believes this originated in the British army around 1900, but it was in general use during the World War II era. Just what is a **brass monkey**? The most persistent and elaborate etymology harks back to the era of wooden ships and iron men, asserting that a **brass monkey** was a device for securing the storage of cannonballs on the gun deck of a man o' war. It is said that cannonballs were stacked up on a square-based pyramid, the top of which had one ball, the next lower level four, the level below that nine, and so on. To keep the bottom level from giving way under the weight of the levels above, a brass plate was laid on deck with a round indentation to accommodate each cannonball of the bottom layer. The brass plate was called a **brass monkey**. Now, brass was used because, unlike iron, it would not rust—and the last thing you wanted was a bunch of iron cannonballs rusted fast to an iron plate. There was, however, one problem. Brass contracts faster than iron, and in very cold weather, the indentations in the **brass monkey** could become smaller than the iron cannonballs resting within them. If the weather got cold enough, the cannonballs would start popping out of the contracting indentations. In other words, it literally was **cold enough to freeze the balls off a brass monkey**.

Few etymologies are more detailed or more persuasive than this one, which is nevertheless a complete fabrication. Cannonballs were never stored stacked up in pyramids on a gun deck, but were carefully stowed in shot lockers below decks. No warship under sail had a brass fitting consisting of a plate with indentations. This leaves open the question of motive. *Why* on earth would someone go through the trouble to concoct so elaborate an explanation of **cold enough to freeze the balls off a brass monkey**? Perhaps the only answer is the one British mountaineer James Mallory reportedly gave when he was asked why he wanted to climb Mount Everest: "Because it's there." The truth is nobody knows why this etymology came into existence any more than anyone knows what, exactly, a brass monkey is.

Variants on the phrase include **cold as a witch's tit** (or **teat**) and **colder than a mother-in-law's breath.**

Crab—Figure out, solve. To **crab** is still a fairly common synonym for *complain*: "All you do is **crab**. If the sun is out, you **crab** about the heat. If it's raining, you **crab** about getting wet." Among tough guys from the 1920s through at least the 1940s, however, the word also meant to figure out or solve. "Your wife and your girl are best friends these days? Buddy, you've got one hell of a problem to **crab**."

Crawler—A double-amputee beggar, especially during the Depression.

Croaker—Physician. In the days before antibiotics, doctors more often presided over sickness than they cured it. People generally consulted a physician only as a last resort. No wonder hardworking folk invented such an unflattering name for the local man of medicine.

Cush—Money, especially the extra money (a "**cush**ion") that might be expected as a result of holding a *cushy job*. That phrase was first heard in Britain during the early twentieth century and drifted across the Atlantic by the end of World War I. **Cush** came into being shortly thereafter.

Damp bourbon poultice—A drink. Laws enacted pursuant to the Eighteenth Amendment prohibiting the manufacture, importation, sale, distribution, and consumption of alcoholic beverages in the United States made an exception for liquor prescribed by a physician for medicinal purposes. Hence the **damp bourbon poultice**—good for what ails you.

Deck—Pack of cigarettes. This was a commonly heard blue-collar term from the 1930s through the 1950s. "Just bought me a **deck** of Luckies." Note that a deck of cards is about the same size and shape as a pack of cigs—and looks the same in shirt pocket.

Diapers—Clothing. To "pin your **diapers** on" is to get dressed. This tough-guy expression was in general use from the 1920s into the World War II era.

Dim box—A taxicab. The expression is reported as current in the 1920s, but its origin is obscure, other than the obvious: A taxi of the era was boxlike and dimly lit.

Dough—Money. This, still the most common vernacular synonym for cash, originated in nineteenth-century America and is almost certainly a reference to **bread**, another slang synonym for cash. **Dough** was sometimes elaborated into **dough-re-mi**, as in "A new Packard? That'll take plenty of **dough-re-mi**."

Both **dough** and **bread** are frequently used in tough-guy fiction and film. Their working-class roots are obvious: Money is equated with survival, the "daily bread" of the Lord's Prayer. Other synonyms in frequent use by the twenties, thirties, forties, and fifties include: **cabbage, clams, coin of the realm, folding stuff, filthy lucre** (from the Bible, 1 Timothy 3:3), **lettuce, long green, jack** (maybe derived from *jackpot*, see chapter One), **mazuma, moolah, plaster, scratch, shekels, spinach**, and **spondilux** (or **spondulix, spondulicks, spondoolicks, spondoolies**—a word that arose in the 1800s, no one knows why). **Greenback** dates to the Civil War, when the term was used to describe the so-called demand notes printed by the U.S. Treasury to help cover the costs of the conflict. The ink used on the backs of these notes was a vivid green; because later U.S. paper currency also used green ink, and the name **greenback** stuck.

Particular denominations of U.S. currency have also attracted a variety of synonyms. A dollar bill is a **buck**. Some authorities trace this term to the mid-eighteenth century, when, on the American frontier, deerskin took on a value in trade that was virtually standardized as a kind of currency. One skin was one **buck** (a buck is a male deer). The money that was subsequently printed in the colonies was more or less pegged to this value and became **bucks**. By the mid-twentieth century, a ten-dollar bill was called a **sawbuck**. This certainly was rooted in **buck**, but no longer simply referred to a male deer. A **sawbuck** is a makeshift device for holding a piece of timber or lumber so that it can be sawed. In its simplest form, it consists of nothing more than two pieces of wood hammered together crosswise, like a big *X*; the lumber to be sawed rests on the joint of the two pieces of wood. Because the Roman numeral for ten is an *X*—and because the Roman numeral was printed on some colonial and nineteenth-century banknotes—the ten-dollar bill became a **sawbuck**. A twenty-dollar bill, Roman numeral *XX*, was designated a **double sawbuck.**

Tough guys also call a ten-dollar bill a **ten-spot** or a **Hamilton** (after the portrait of Alexander Hamilton that appears on the note). A five-dollar bill is a **fin** or **five-spot**. No self-respecting gangster would ever ask another for the loan of a five or a ten, but would instead say, "Can you **spot** me five or ten?" The twenty may be called a **Jackson**, and the hundred a **Franklin**, **Benjamin**, or even **Benji** (after the engraved portraits, respectively, of Andrew Jackson and Benjamin Franklin). The two-dollar bill, common in the tough-guy era but now scarce, was a **deuce** and, less often, a **Jefferson**, or a **TJ** (Thomas Jefferson adorns the note).

The hundred-dollar bill loomed large in the 1920s and 1930s as a **C-note** (*C* being the Roman numeral for *100*), a **century note**, or even just a **bill** (five **bills** is five hundred dollars). The U.S. Treasury stopped issuing currency in denominations above $100 in 1946, and notes in denominations of $500, $1,000, $5,000, $10,000, and $100,000 were withdrawn from circulation in 1969. Gangsters called the $1,000 bill a **large**, and, even today, units of a thousand dollars are sometimes spoken of as **large**: "He owes me fifty **large**"—$50,000.

Dogs are barkin', my—My feet are sore (from walking, standing, or working all day). The use of **dogs** as a synonym for *feet* has been recorded in print at least as early as 1913 in a story published by T. A. Dorgan in the *New York Evening Journal* that year; a character complains that he is "waitin' for my sore **dog** to heal up." As early as 1914, **dogs** was used as a synonym for *shoes*. The *Oxford English Dictionary* finds the earliest use of **dogs** meaning *feet* in 1924, but a *Ladies Home Journal* article from 1919 observes that a "marine never calls a foot anything but a **dog**." During the ragtime era, which began in the late 1890s and extended through World War I, it was common to invite a dancing partner to "shake her/his **dogs**."

Ducat—Ticket. Popular among show people and their audience early in the twentieth century, the word originally described an Italian gold coin first issued by Roger II of Sicily (1095–1154) in 1140 and still in use up to World War I (1914–1918). By the sixteenth century, the **ducat** was adopted throughout Europe as the standard gold coin. Doubtless, the similarity in sound between **ducat** and *ticket* is the source of **ducat**'s use as an informal synonym. Broadway took up the word early in the twentieth century. During the 1920s, a **ducat** was also a printed card that street beggars showed to passersby; such cards explained that the bearer was blind, or deaf, or mute, or in some other way disabled and therefore in need of charity.

Egg in your beer (What do you want?)—"What more do you want?" Or "Don't you have it good enough already?" Old-time bartenders are not surprised by a customer's request for egg in his beer, since a raw egg cracked into a beer was long considered a hangover cure. The phrase **egg in your beer** probably dates from the nineteenth century, but it became popular during World War II when wartime rationing made both eggs and beer scarce commodities. You might expect to have one or the other, but not both.

Shop steward: "I got you a nickel more an hour."

Worker: "What about that extra fifteen minutes for lunch we asked for?"

Shop steward: "Whadda ya want, **egg in your beer**?"

See **eggs in the coffee**.

Eggs in the coffee—Easy, simple, a cinch. More obscure than **egg in your beer**, this expression is roughly the equivalent of *a piece of cake*. Cowboys traditionally prepared coffee with eggshells in the bottom of the cup to settle the grounds. The novelist John Steinbeck (1902–1968) described preparing coffee by cracking an egg, cupping out the yolk, and dropping "white and shells into the pot" because "nothing [else] polishes coffee and makes it shine like that." Other folks believe in reserving the yolk, dropping it into the cup, then pouring the coffee over it. The question, of course, is why the **eggs in the coffee** procedure should have become a synonym for easy, simple, a cinch. Those who like eggs in their coffee (and their number seems to be diminishing) point out that it makes even the strongest cup slide down smooth. If this suggests ease and simplicity, then the source of the expression may have been found.

Give (or **gave**) **me the buzz**—Come (or came) calling at my door. From the 1950s on, the phrase **give me a buzz** was generally understood to mean *please call me on the telephone*. During the 1920s–1940s, however, people were generally more careful with their language. A request for a phone call was **give me a ring** or **ring me** or **ring me up**, whereas an invitation to drop by the apartment was **give me a buzz**, the idea being that a phone rang and an apartment buzzer—well, buzzed. "Mabel **gave me a buzz** last night. We had a good time, a *very* good time."

Hobo Short Line, the—Suicide committed by throwing oneself in front of a train. The phrase came about in the 1930s, when tens of thousands of out-of-work itinerants rode the rails. As anyone who has played Monopoly knows, the Short Line was a real railroad.

Hooverville—A shantytown or communal camp-site occupied by squatters during the Great Depression. The name derived from Republican president Herbert Hoover (1874–1964), whose economic policies were widely blamed for the economic crisis. The label was not spontaneously affixed by a disillusioned public but was the invention of Charles Michelson, the publicity director of the Democratic National Committee. It stuck and helped ensure that Hoover would be a one-term president.

How's tricks?—How are things going? Or, more simply: How are you? Common by the 1920s. Aware that a *trick* is the client of a prostitute, one might assume that a vulgar impertinence is cloaked in this apparently friendly greeting; however, *The Oxford English Dictionary* contends that the phrase derives not from the world's oldest profession but from the special vocabulary of sailors: A "trick" is a turn ("watch") at the helm, so this is an inquiry as to whether one's watch has been eventful, uneventful, difficult, or easy.

Kibitzer—A person who stands on the sidelines and delivers unsolicited and usually annoying advice; a sidewalk superintendent. The word is a borrowing from the Yiddish *Kiebitz*, meaning "peewit" or "lapwing," a small, noisy, and annoying bird. The "business" of a **kibitzer** is to **kibitz**. Note that the connotation is not always totally negative. A sports fan might actually boast that he "enjoys **kibitzing** a baseball game."

Knuckle buster—A mechanic. During World War II, the vehicle mechanics who worked in an army motor pool and the aircraft mechanics in the U.S. Army Air Forces were universally dubbed **knuckle busters**. The name derived from the condition of the mechanic's knuckles, skinned and raw from when the wrench slipped on the nut, causing him to scrape his knuckles.

Make my (your) nut—Earn enough to pay one's expenses for a given period: "I need $500 each and every month just to **make my nut**." In use by the 1930s, still popular well into the 1950s, and even heard today, this phrase invites thoughts of the prudent squirrel who stores nuts for the winter, but in fact originated in early nineteenth-century England and refers not to the nut from which a tree may grow but the piece of hardware that keeps the wheels from falling off the wagon. Itinerant gypsy bands would travel from town to town, offering entertainment to the provinces but also bringing the scourge of petty crime—pickpocketing, flimflamming, and the like. The town fathers would meet the gypsies upon their arrival and negotiate the amount of the sum due the town in return for the privilege of doing business. As security against payment of the agreed-on fee, the sheriff would take possession of the nut that kept the biggest wheel affixed to the axle of the biggest circus wagon. Only after the circus people paid the agreed-on fee would the sheriff return the hardware. It would be awfully dicey for the circus to steal away under cover of darkness if a wheel fell off the wagon. Until they **made their nut**, they weren't going anywhere.

Moxie—Courage, guts, energy, daring, spunk. "That guy, he's got **moxie**." Moxie was introduced in 1876 as a patent medicine called Moxie Nerve Food and advertised as a cure for "paralysis, softening of the brain, nervousness, and insomnia." By 1884, Moxie was being sold as a bottled carbonated beverage. Thanks to an intensive advertising campaign, it became extremely popular in the 1920s, but began a long decline in the 1930s. Yet it manages to survive. As a synonym for *spunk*, *guts*, and *get-up-and-go*, **moxie** was born of the beverage's 1920s-era advertising, which was sufficiently pervasive to penetrate the American language.

One thin dime—An inconsiderable sum of money; used to persuade a prospective buyer that proffered merchandise is a great bargain. The phrase is associated with the itinerant salesmen, street peddlers, hawkers of patent medicines, and carnival barkers who operated in an era when many products were priced at a dime. Although a dime is hardly the least amount of money one can spend (there are nickels and pennies, after all), it is physically the thinnest (and smallest) U.S. coin. "Here it is, ladies and gentlemen—Kickapoo Indian Sagwa, the blood, liver, and stomach renovator, twelve ounces of rejuvenation, all yours for **one thin dime**!"

The catchphrase was also used as a synonym for being broke: "I haven't got **one thin dime** to my name!" Alternatively: "I don't have **two nickels to rub together**."

Peddle your papers—Go away and mind your own business. Born of an era in which newsboys sold newspapers on street corners, this has been around at least since the 1920s; however, it gained popularity in the 1930s and was widely used by tough guys through the 1940s. In the 1947 film noir *Kiss of Death*, Victor Mature (as ex-con Nick Bianco) tells hoodlum Tommy Udo (played by Richard Widmark in his film debut), "Go on, beat it! **Peddle your papers**." Because the phrase is figuratively addressed to a newsboy—a kid—it is emphatically dismissive. Udo/Widmark was not one to be demeaned, however, and shocked filmgoers in a later scene by tying an old lady to her wheelchair and pushing her down a flight of tenement stairs. (She dies.)

Strike a blow for liberty—Have a sociable drink. The phrase was made famous by Senator (later Vice President and President) Harry S. Truman (1884–1972), beginning about 1937 when he was serving in the Senate. It described the ritual of top Democratic politicians gathering for a drink at the end of the day in the Capitol office of Representative Sam Rayburn (1882–1961), who was majority leader from 1937 to 1940 and Speaker of the House during 1940–1947, 1949–1953, and 1955–1961. Raising his glass, Truman would pose the rhetorical question, "Shall we **strike a blow for liberty**, gentlemen?"

Take it on the arches—Depart, leave, exit, move along, scram. Before the 1960s, most jobs put you on your feet and not behind a cushy desk. Many a working man and woman suffered the agony of what was commonly known as "flat feet" or "fallen arches"—*pes planus* (in medical parlance), a condition in which the arch or instep of the foot comes in contact with the ground. A **working stiff** afflicted with fallen arches was always looking for an opportunity to take a load off, but when he sat somewhere long enough to look like a Depression-era loiterer or **bindle stiff**, there always seemed to be a cop nearby to advise him to **take it on the arches**, meaning to get up and start walking.

Take the pipe—Commit suicide. The phrase was current by 1949 (and probably long before), when Arthur Miller (1915–2005) alluded to it in his play *Death of a Salesman*, in which protagonist Willy Loman contemplates killing himself by attaching a rubber hose to the pipe that supplies gas to his home. Although the phrase specifically refers to suicide by natural gas inhalation, it was used as a synonym for suicide by any means.

Three squares—Three "square meals" a day; used to describe the minimum standard for subsistence. "Times is tough. All I need is a job that'll get me my **three squares**" (or, **three squares a day**). See **three hots and a cot**.

Tin Pan Alley—The American popular music industry as it existed from the late nineteenth century through the 1920s. The music publishers who constituted most of this industry were located on or near Manhattan's Seventh Avenue between 48th and 52nd streets, a neighborhood that came to be called **Tin Pan Alley** after the ceaseless tinkling of mass-produced melody from tinny pianos (called **pans** by the musicians who played them) that emerged from the many purveyors of popular music. Merely geographically descriptive when the phrase was first used, **Tin Pan Alley** became a derisive label for the cliché-ridden musical fodder ground out during much of the ragtime and early jazz eras. See **Tinseltown**.

Tinseltown—Somewhat playfully derisive synonym for Hollywood, California. The word *tinsel* has been used to describe anything glittering and showy but without intrinsic worth since the seventeenth century, and it was applied to shiny metallic decoration, such as that used in brocade work, a century before that. Most of us know the word as the name of the cheap metallic stuff used to decorate Christmas trees. In any of these senses, *tinsel* is an apt term to apply to Hollywood, the seat of the American film industry, which so often trades on glittering but empty dreams and whose celebrities sparkle but—often enough—lack substance. Given the venerable origin of *tinsel*, we could be forgiven for assuming that **Tinseltown** must date to the beginnings of Hollywood as a film capital in the 1910s just as **Tin Pan Alley** dates to the heyday of Seventh Avenue in Midtown Manhattan as the capital of American popular music at about that same time. Forgiven we might be, but the assumption is wrong nevertheless. The term **Tinseltown** first appeared in print during the 1970s.

To beat the band—To go all out; to make the most impressive effort or showing. Current by the 1910s, this expression may have originated in the world of popular entertainment. The best singer was the loudest singer, the volume of whose voice was sufficient **to beat the band**—that is, to be heard above the level of the musical accompaniment. The saying may be related to the somewhat-earlier **to beat the Dutch**, which, as near as anyone can figure out today, meant presenting something convincing enough to impress even a "Dutchman" (the word most Americans applied to Germans), a member of a nationality perceived as very difficult to persuade.

Visiting fireman—A VIP visitor to the office or workplace, whom one is obliged to show around or otherwise entertain. The implication is that the visit is a more or less unwelcome interruption in the workday. The phrase was first reported in 1926, and although it is natural to assume that it originated in the visit of an out-of-town firefighter or fire chief to a local firehouse, the distinguished American student of slang, Dr. Robert L. Chapman, believes that the "fireman" in this phrase refers to a Native American ceremonial figure who was responsible for lighting sacred or celebratory fires.

Walking papers—Pink slip; dismissal from employment or from a romantic engagement: "The boss handed me my **walking papers** yesterday." This expression was heard a whole lot during the Great Depression of the 1930s, and it's still heard a whole lot today. It appeared in print, in the sense of the termination of a romantic engagement, in 1825: "As for the bumpkin, her lover, he must take his **walking papers**" (Samuel Woodworth, *Forest Rose, or, American Farmers*).

White-shoe—Elite, elitist, Ivy League. During the 1920s, **white-shoe** was used as an adjective to describe any elite person, organization, or attitude. The phrase survives to describe conservative, elite professions, especially law firms. During the 1920s, students in Ivy League colleges often wore white buck shoes.

Whole ball of wax—The sum, the totality, everything, the entire thing. The phrase emerged in the 1950s but appeared in print at least as early April 25, 1882, when *The Atlanta Journal-Constitution* used the expression in a story about auction sales by realtor John Sherman & Co.: "We will be greatly surprised if Mr. Sherman does not attempt to sell out the **whole ball of wax** under the hammer." Over the years, scholars and others have taken many stabs at assigning an origin to the phrase. The three most prominent theories:

1) It originated with workers in London's famed Madame Tussaud's Wax Museum, to describe a certain process of readying wax.

2) Old-time typesetters who employed gold in casting type (did they really?) would use a ball of wax to collect gold flakes from their equipment for recycling; sometimes workers would steal the **whole ball of wax**.

3) An English law text from 1620 outlines a lottery for allocating land among the heirs to an estate in the absence of a will; each portion of land was to be listed on a separate piece of paper, each piece was to be sealed into a small ball of wax and placed in a hat, and each heir was to draw one ball of wax to discover his portion. It is this third candidate that is most widely cited today as the source of the expression, even though it is both very remote in time and place from the principal users of the expression and even though it makes very little sense. The lottery specified in the English text describes a number of small, individual wax balls, not the *whole* ball of wax.

Perhaps the most plausible origin is in another, more recent British expression, the *whole bailiwick*, which some American transformed into the **whole ball of**

wax simply because it sounded funny. The fact is that **whole ball of wax** is only one of a number of similar expressions that rose to their greatest popularity during the 1940s and 1950s, including the **whole enchilada**, **whole megillah**, **whole nine yards**, and, perhaps the granddaddy of them all, the **whole shebang** (see all).

Whole enchilada—One of a number of similar expressions meaning the sum, the totality, everything, the entire thing. This seems to have emerged in the 1950s and to have lingered through new generations of users. No one knows where it came from, but we can guess that someone, somewhere, sometime got tired of saying the **whole ball of wax** and substituted a tasty specimen of Mexican cuisine. In this, hunger may have played as important a role as imagination.

Whole megillah—Yet another way of saying the whole thing, the totality; however, the **whole megillah** has the added connotation of burden: "There are taxes to pay, estate taxes, sales taxes, transfer taxes, income taxes—the **whole megillah**." (Contrast: "There are profits to be made, royalties, licensing fees rental fees—the **whole enchilada**.") "Megillah" is another American borrowing from the vast linguistic trove that is Yiddish—though, in this case, Yiddish is merely the vessel that carried the original Hebrew word, *megillah*, which translates roughly as *scroll* and is used as a synonym for any one of the following five books of the Old Testament: *Song of Songs, book of Ruth, Lamentations, Ecclesiastes*, and *book of Esther*. Even more specifically, *megillah* was used most frequently to refer to *Esther*, which is supposed to be read *in its totality* on the feast of Purim. Doubtless, many of the faithful were daunted by the prospect of sitting through a reading of *that* **whole megillah**.

Whole nine yards—Sum, totality, everything, but with the added implication of making an extra effort or (to shift units of measurement), going the extra mile. It is widely assumed that this phrase came into use at about the same time as most of the other "whole" phrases were heard: **whole ball of wax**, whole megillah, and so on; however, researchers have identified only one recorded instance of **whole nine yards** used before the 1960s. We'll get to that in a moment, but despite an absence of printed evidence, this phrase has been the subject of extensive, even desperate, etymological speculation. Some insist that it is a reference to the yardage of material used to make a nun's habit, a standard three-piece suit, or an Indian maharajah's sash. Others say that nine yards is the length of a standard hangman's rope. Still others insist that it has more to do with avoiding the hangman's rope in the first place, the **whole nine yards** being the standard length from the cellblock to the outer wall of a prison and, therefore, the distance a condemned man would have to run to make good an escape. Failing in this attempt, you would find yourself wound in the standard nine-yard shroud for burial.

What else? "Nine yards" has been cited as standard material for a Scotsman's kilt, for the cloth that goes into making a soldier's backpack, and even as a key measurement in football. The problem is that none of these standards is standard—not even remotely. Even the best-dressed nun wears nothing approaching nine yards of cloth, and a man's three-piece suit requires no more than five square yards of material. As for football, the basic unit for scoring is ten yards (that gets you a first down), whereas going the **whole nine yards** gets you nothing.

There are more guesses, ranging from obscure references to yardarms of sailing ships and the length of ammunition belts for .50-cal machine guns in World War II U.S. bombers. The fact is that nobody knows where the expression came from; however, the earliest *attested* use of the phrase was identified by Barry Popik, a New York–based etymologist and contributor to *The Oxford English Dictionary*, who related a story heard by U.S. Navy captain Richard Stratton at the Naval Air Station in Pensacola, Florida, in July 1955. It was the tale of one Andrew MacTavish who courted Margaret Mary MacDuff. MacTavish knit a scarf for Margaret Mary, intending to give it to her as a birthday present. He knitted like mad, not stopping until he had produced nine gaudy yards.

Having finished the scarf, he donned his kilt, wrapped the scarf around his neck, and popped down to the pub for a drink with the boys. More than *a* drink, naturally. As everyone descended more deeply into their cups, some unkind words began to fly concerning the merits of what was, after all, a very ugly scarf. His confidence shaken, a sodden MacTavish walked through the late-night gloom to Margaret Mary's house with the intention of asking her opinion of the gift *before* he gave it to her. In the course of a long, rough, rural walk, MacTavish retained the scarf but lost his kilt, so that when he arrived below his sweetheart's window and succeeded in waking her by throwing gravel against the glass, he was quite naked, save for the scarf.

He was also greatly cheered by the prospect of seeing Margaret Mary. *Greatly* cheered.

The sleepy girl opened her window and beheld her fiancé, greatly cheered as he was.

"Margaret Mary, I have made this just for you. I'm going to give it to you on your birthday. How do you like it?"

The girl was not looking at the scarf when she managed to reply, "Just fine, Andy dear, just fine. It is magnificent."

Wanting to make absolutely sure, MacTavish called back to her: "The **whole nine yards**?"

Whole schmear (or **schmeer**)—Sum, totality, everything, complete. Order a bagel and cream cheese in an old-school New York deli, and you'll be asked if you want a "slab or a **schmear**," the cream cheese laid down in a slab or spread flat in a schmear. Quite possibly, **whole schmear** comes from this usage of the word. Many authorities, however, believe it is a reference to the Yiddish verb *schmeeren*, which is used to describe spreading out one's hand (of cards) in a game of pinochle or gin rummy. The player thus reveals his **whole schmear**.

Whole shebang—Sum, totality, everything, complete. Whereas **whole schmear** borrows from America's Yiddish-speaking immigrants, **whole shebang** takes from an even earlier group of arrivals, the Irish, and the first recorded use of the expression was in 1869. A *shebang* is a hovel or shanty and is almost certainly derived from the Irish word *shebeen,* meaning something like "cheap saloon." Thus the **whole shebang** is the whole house (such as it is) and everything inside it (such as it is).

Whole shooting (or **shootin'**) match—Sum, totality, everything, complete—with the added implication that this totality constitutes something at stake.

Q: "You're betting your whole bankroll on this *one* horse?"

A: "The **whole shooting match**."

Often, the expression is used after a loss: "Well, there goes the **whole shootin' match**."

Win the porcelain helmet (or **hairnet**)—Receive something useless or of highly dubious value. Heard chiefly during the 1930s, with variants including **win the barbwire garter** and **win the fur-lined bathtub**. To wear a porcelain helmet may also suggest getting something worse than useless, such as a toilet for a hat. One of the characters on the police drama *Hill Street Blues*, which aired on NBC from 1981 to 1987, an uptight SWAT commander, characterized the embarrassment of failure as **wearing the brown helmet**, which may well have been a variant of the 1930s expression.

Wood pusher—A clerk, bookkeeper, or any other person with a desk job; a pencil pusher. The term, popular beginning in the 1920s and persisting today, is often used as a synonym for *bureaucrat* or any other worker whose job tends to multiply red tape rather than actually accomplish anything.

Working stiff—An ordinary workingman (or woman), typically employed in a routine, dead-end blue-collar job. Modern dictionaries define *stiff*, at least in this context, as a synonym for *fellow* or even *person*; however, the association of *stiff* with *corpse* is unmistakable, and the implication is that an ordinary workingman, a **working stiff**, is a kind of wage zombie. Compare **lucky stiff**, a person whose good fortune is not the result of anything done to earn it. If the **working stiff** is a wage zombie, the **lucky stiff** is a zombie of fortune.

By the 1950s, when many young people (especially men returning from military service) were moved to create a career rather than simply hold a job, the title **working stiff** was sometimes adopted as a perverse emblem of pride, evidence that one knew who one was and was happy with it: "College? Why should *I* go to college. I'm a **working stiff**, and I'll always be a **working stiff**."

Yenems—Somebody else's (Yiddish). American English has borrowed a great many words from the Yiddish language, particularly during the era of massive immigration from Eastern Europe at the end of the nineteenth century and beginning of the twentieth. **Yenems** entered working-class vocabulary during the late 1910s and faded away by the era of World War II. It refers to anything that belongs to someone else, but that you use.

Q: "How do you make a living?"
A: "I invest."
Q: "With what money?"
A: "**Yenems**." (That is, other people's money.)

Yes, we have no bananas—A way of saying no when you'd like to be able to say yes. This reply is actually the first line of the refrain from the song of the same name by **Tin Pan Alley**'s Frank Silver and Irving Cohn, published in 1923. In 1953, the dean of American slang studies, Professor Eric Partridge, offered documentary proof that these five words (or seven syllables) constituted the most widely used popular catchphrase in the United States from 1923 to 1927, and the humorist Will Rogers (1879–1935) declared, "I would rather have been the Author of that Banana Masterpiece than the Author of the Constitution of the United States," adding, "No one has offered any amendments to it." It should be noted, however, that Silver and Cohn followed their 1923 hit three years later with "I've Never Seen a Straight Banana," a song publicized in London with an offer of £1,000 to anyone who could produce such a specimen of the fruit. To this very day, no one has come forward to claim the prize.

Hardware store customer: Do you carry left-handed monkey wrenches?

Hardware store owner: **Yes, we have no bananas.**

You scratch my back, I'll scratch yours—Quid pro quo, vernacular version. This homely negotiation—help me, and I'll help you, or let's help each other—may be traced to the seventeenth-century proverbial proposition, *scratch my breech, and I'll claw your elbow* (breech = buttocks). In British English, the proverbial expression survives as an invitation to exchange compliments: *You flatter me, and I'll flatter you.* Compare this to *One hand washes the other*, which (by the early twentieth century) was often followed by *and both hands wash the face.* Thus, not only can we help each other out, but, by cooperating, achieve something even greater.

SIX

Four-Flushers, Two-Timers, Bad Eggs, and Egg Suckers

When Invective Was Really Effective

lderman—A man's potbelly. This is a splendid example of what rhetoricians call metonymy: a figure of speech in which a concept or a thing is not directly named but is identified by naming something closely associated with it. Just as *the Crown* is another way of saying *the king* (a crown is closely associated with a king), so **alderman** (a middle-aged man whose fat belly is the product of high living fueled by bribes) is a way of saying *potbelly*. In the exuberantly corrupt world of 1920s urban American politics, this must have led to some interesting exchanges, such as "Get a load of the **alderman** on our mayor!" or even, "Must have been a good year. The alderman's grown quite an **alderman**."

Alibi Ike—A screwup who never lacks for (implausible) excuses. This is one of those rare tough-guy expressions traceable to a specific source, namely the "Alibi Ike" stories of sports writer and brilliantly colloquial short-fiction satirist Ringgold Wilmer "Ring" Lardner (1885–1933). Published serially in *The Saturday Evening Post* beginning on July 31, 1915, the stories narrate the exploits of one Frank X. Farrell, a fictional professional baseball player probably based on King Cole, who pitched for the Chicago Cubs, Pittsburgh Pirates (briefly), and the New York Yankees. Cole was a favorite subject of Lardner the sports columnist, and the Alibi Ike stories began to appear during what would prove Cole's final season. Diagnosed with tuberculosis in 1915, he died early the following year at the age of twenty-nine.

The odd thing is that, like King Cole, Lardner's Alibi Ike was anything but a loser, yet he couldn't resist making up excuses for virtually *everything* that happened, good or bad. For instance, he "blamed" a spectacular .356 batting average on having "come down with malaria" that season. As the expression **Alibi Ike** entered the language and became popular—boosted by a 1935 movie, *Alibi Ike*, starring gate-mouth comedian Joe E. Brown and stunner Olivia de Haviland—it invariably described a poor slob who lived by excuses (and had ample need to do so).

Bad egg—A criminal or other malefactor. A **bad egg** is a rotten egg—or a rotten human being. The phrase dates from the nineteenth century and resurfaced with a vengeance during the lawless Roaring Twenties.

Baumes rush, the—A life sentence via New York State's 1926 four-strikes law. Three-strikes laws are a relatively recent phenomenon, but the legislated mandatory life sentence upon a *fourth* felony conviction was born back in 1926, at the height of the national crime wave created by Prohibition, which transformed a perpetually thirsty America into a nation of lawbreakers willing to tolerate organized crime as long as it kept the hooch coming. State senator Caleb H. Baumes (1863–1937), chair of the New York State Crime Commission, wrote the law and championed its passage. Any defendant who received a fourth felony conviction was given **the Baumes rush**: doomed to spend the rest of his or her life in prison, whether the crime was murder or, in the infamous case of one Ruth St. Clair, shoplifting. The phrase is a play on being "given the bum's rush," a catchphrase (still in use, if somewhat archaic) meaning unceremonious, even forcible, ejection, as a deadbeat might be ushered out of a fancy restaurant. Baumes's law served as a model for other states, twenty-three of which enacted similar legislation by the end of the Roaring Twenties.

Beeswax, mind your own—Mind your own business. This invitation to buzz off, a deliberately comic malapropism, is noted as early as 1934 in Jonathan Lighter's *Historical Dictionary of American Slang* (1994). Presumably the comic element was intended to blunt the hard edge of the more direct demand to *mind your own business.*

Bimbo—Originally (that is, from about 1910), a menacing man, likely engaged in criminal activity. Detective fiction master Dashiell Hammett described "**bimbos** [who] once helped pluck a bank." Only after 1920 was **bimbo** more commonly used to describe a young woman, especially one of questionable virtue, if not an outright prostitute. By early in the twentieth century, the word was also used to describe anyone insignificant, regardless of gender.

That this word should encompass such a range of meanings—from thugs, to women, to prostitutes, to nonentities—is remarkable, especially considering its origin in the Italian *bambino* (baby) and the proper noun derived from *bambino*, *Bimbo*, which was a common name Italian organ grinders applied to their monkeys and which was also applied to children's dolls modeled after these monkeys.

Bogart—As used by African Americans in the 1940s, to behave in a surly or intimidating manner; as used by connoisseurs of cannabis, regardless of race, to hog a shared joint; by extension, to take more than one's fair share of anything. For both senses of the word, the source is film noir tough guy Humphrey Bogart (1899–1957), who not only projected iconic onscreen images of underworld intimidation but cupped his cigarette in a manner (mouth end pinched between thumb and middle and forefingers, flame end held within the arched palm) that became a kind of personal trademark. While the actor's tough-guy image gave birth to the verb **Bogart** as a synonym for *menace* or *intimidate*, his way with a smoke suggested an acute appetite, both surreptitious and rapacious, for whatever was rolled into a cigarette.

Butter and egg man, big—A rich rube; that is, a fool from whom money is easily parted; sometimes more specifically, a bumpkin who comes to the city and blows his bankroll on women and nightclubs. The phrase entered mainstream American English via playwright George S. Kaufman's 1925 Broadway comic hit *The Butter and Egg Man,* about a wealthy hick who is taken by an unscrupulous Broadway producer to finance a flop (anticipating Mel Brooks's *The Producers*, both movie and musical, by many decades) but who ends up having the last laugh. In 1928, the play was made into a First National Pictures silent movie (starring, as hayseed Jack McClure, William Demarest, better known to somewhat more modern audiences for playing Uncle Charley on TV's *My Three Sons* from 1965 to 1972). Just a year after the Kaufman play premiered, songwriter Percy Venable was inspired to write "Big Butter and Egg Man," which was a big hit for Louis Armstrong.

Although Kaufman's play popularized the phrase, it was the celebrated Prohibition-era speakeasy hostess Texas Guinan (1884–1933) who actually invented it. She liked to tell the story of a "man with a slow Midwestern drawl" who ambled into her El Fey Club one evening and immediately bought everyone a drink. Tex escorted her generous guest to the center of the dance floor, signaled for a drum roll, and ceremoniously introduced him to her patrons as "a live one, a buyer, a good guy, a sport of the old school, encourage him." When Tex asked him his name, he replied, "Nix on the name." When she persisted, "What's your racket, then?" he muttered, "I'm a big man in dairy produce."

"That's applesauce to this mob," she told him. "I'll send you right in." Then, turning to the nightclubbers, she triumphantly proclaimed: "He's a **big butter and egg man**."

The expression spread throughout Manhattan, Kaufman picked it up, wrote his play, and broadcast it to the world.

Clothesline—A gossip or rumormonger; also applied to the article of gossip itself. The idea here is that neighbor ladies gossip with one another over the clothesline while hanging or collecting the wash.

Cracked in the right place—Wisegal's reply to "You must be cracked." A tough guy of the 1930s–1940s never called a woman crazy. He told her she was "cracked," as in cracked in the head. If a girl possessed enough sass, she'd reply, "Yes, **cracked in the right place**." Depending on the tone in which it was delivered, this was definitely dismissive or provocatively flirtatious. (Etymologist Eric Partridge reported first hearing the phrase not in the United States, but in England, and not in the thirties or forties, but in 1922, which was at the height of post–World War I sexual liberation.)

Dead but he won't lie down—Really, really dense, as in *How dense can one person be?* The catchphrase was certainly current as of about 1910, but it was a wisecrack heard all the way through the World War II era. "Mickey? Mickey invested all his **dough** with that guy Ponzi they put away in November. Even so, Mick's still waiting for his dividend check. Thing about Mickey is, he's **dead but he won't lie down**."

Dewdropper—Loafer or malingerer. Reported in the 1940s. This one is rare, and no authority seems to have made a stab at the term's origin. We can guess. Anyone who takes an early-morning stroll discovers dewdrops on the grass, leaves, and other motionless specimens of flora and fauna, presumably including a loafer or malingerer, who is sufficiently idle to collect dew. It is also possible that the word is related to the British euphemism for a drop of mucus hanging from one's nose—a **dewdrop**—suggesting a person too lazy even to blow or wipe his nose.

Don't hand me that line!—Don't try to bullshit me. The word *line* suggests a memorized speech (as in an actor's *line*) or an official position (the party *line*); therefore, to **hand one a line** is to say something that is insincere or patently untrue. Typically, the sentence is used in response to an excuse perceived as implausible or unworthy of credibility. Recorded in the early 1900s, the sentence figures in the speech of many a tough guy and tough gal through the 1950s.

Drink out of the same bottle—Are close friends. You drink out of the bottle only among friends; you **drink out of the same bottle** only with a very close friend. The origin of the phrase is unknown.

Dumb Dora—A really stupid woman: "She's the original **Dumb Dora**." Although some authorities trace the phrase to 1910–1915, it became widespread with a 1920s fad for Dumb Dora jokes, formulaic gags that always began "Dora was so dumb that . . . " then continued with the likes of "she thought a subordinate clause was Santa's son" or "asphalt is a disease of the rectum."

Egg sucker—An alternative way of calling a person a weasel. Weasels are notorious for raiding chicken coops and hen houses where they supposedly suck the white and yolk out of eggs. In fact, although weasels do eat eggs, they lack the kind of jaw and mouthparts needed to suck them. No matter, the idea is that, as the animal weasel sucks the "meat" out of an egg, leaving only an empty shell, so the human weasel sucks the meaning out words, using them in ways that evade taking a meaningful stand. Often, **egg sucker** is used as a synonym for an empty flatterer, a brown nose.

Fart's the cry of an imprisoned turd—An excuse for breaking wind in company. First recorded in the early 1930s, it is a lyrical alternative to saying nothing in the hope that nobody has noticed. From the same decade on a similar theme, this couplet:

Better to belch and bear the shame
Than not to belch and bear the pain.

Fifty cards in the deck—Not playing with a full deck; that is, crazy. The still-current expression **not**

playing with a full deck has been dated to circa 1930, the year Dashiell Hammett published *The Maltese Falcon*, in which **hard-boiled** private eye Sam Spade wonders, "How do you figure her? Only **fifty cards in her deck**?" A standard full deck has fifty-two playing cards.

For the man who has everything—An unwanted gift or a purported asset that is actually a liability. Born in advertising of the 1950s, when the most pressing problem a suburban housewife faced (other than a chronic sense of desolation and despair) was what to get her white-collar husband for Christmas, the phrase was quickly transformed into world-weary irony, as in, "So now it turns out I've got hemorrhoids. Oh well, what do you get **for the man who has everything**?"

Four-flusher—A cheat or swindler; sometimes used to describe a braggart or bluffer. The root of this specimen of invective, which dates to the late nineteenth century, is found in the game of poker; however, while **four-flusher** is usually intended as a synonym for cheater, to *four-flush* in poker is not, in fact, to cheat but to pull off a brazen bluff by trying to convince the other players that you hold a full flush when you are actually one card short (and hold only a **four-flush**). Those who use **four-flusher** as a synonym for *braggart* or *bluffer* rather than *cheater* remain closer to the spirit of the word.

Funny as a crutch—Not at all funny. The phrase had its origin in the 1930s. A somewhat-softened version of it runs **funny as a rubber crutch.**

Would-be comic: OK. Here's a good one. Guy goes to his doctor. There's a cucumber in one ear, a pickle in the other, and a string bean up each nostril. "Doc," he says, "what's wrong with me?" Doctor answers, "I don't think you're eating properly."

(*Pause*)

Critic: Ugh. **Funny as a crutch**.

Get wise to yourself!—Don't be ridiculous! Phrases built on a core of **get wise**, **get wise to**, and **wise up** liberally pepper tough-guy talk in novels and films of the 1930s and 1940s; however **get wise to yourself!** goes back at least as far as the 1910s. See also **hurry up and get born!**

Go find a drum and beat it!—Get lost, take a hike, go away. An elaboration of the old standby *beat it*.

Hurry up and get born!—You're way behind the times. Get with it! Another abrasive retort worthy of a wiseacre of the 1930s and 1940s, the phrase is believed to date from the 1910s and was reported in print in 1919 by a London journalist who identified it as an American import.

Meanwhile, back at the ranch . . . —Used to prod a tediously meandering speaker back to the subject at hand or the point he was apparently about to make; the equivalent of *Get to the point already, will you?* Origin: the era of silent-film Westerns. When the plot would shift from a desperate gunfight in progress to a scene in which Little Nell is menaced by Black Bart back at the ranch, a title would flash on the screen to signal the shift in location: **Meanwhile, back at the ranch . . .**

Doddering speaker: The next part is very important. In fact, it's the key that will open all doors for you. But, speaking of keys, did I ever tell you about the time *blah blah blah . . . and blah blah blah . . .*

Exasperated listener: **Meanwhile, back at the ranch . . .**

Pantywaist—A weak, effeminate man; a sissy. The word was first used in this sense in the 1930s and endured at least through the 1950s. Although *panty* suggests a female undergarment, the term comes most directly from a child's garment actually called a pantywaist, which consisted of short *pants* buttoned to the *waist* of a shirt and popular in the 1920s and 1930s. "Don't apologize for making him cry. He's a **pantywaist** anyway."

Popular as a pork chop at synagogue—Highly unwelcome. This example was reported in the 1950s, during which **(as) popular as a turd on a lunch**

counter and **(it) went over like a lead balloon** were also frequently used.

Sad sack—An awkward, unfortunate, maladroit person. The term is documented as early as the 1920s but came into its greatest popularity during World War II. In a strictly military context (U.S. Army), it was used to describe an officer who had a penchant for making the already-burdensome military life even more burdensome, and gratuitously so, usually by a pedantic adherence to "the Book" (military regulations). Its civilian application is far less specific (see **zhlub**). "My brother in law, if it were raining soup, would run outside with a fork. He's a real **sad sack**, he is."

Take a long walk on a short pier, go and—Bon voyage with extreme prejudice, or, more gently, please go away and don't bother me. Of the same vintage and with the same meaning as **Go peddle your papers**.

Panhandler: "Brother, can you spare a dime?"

Passerby: Why don't you **go and take a long walk on a short pier**.

Take a powder—Can be used as an imperative *go away, scram, take a hike*, or merely as a description of an action: "I gotta **take a powder**" (leave) or "He **took a powder**" (left suddenly, with the implication of having walked out on some responsibility). Although this is one of the most common phrases in the dialogue of tough-guy novels and movies, its origin is obscure.

The common-sense etymology is the woman who excused herself momentarily from a dinner or social gathering by announcing that she has to *powder her nose* (i.e., go to the bathroom). In more than a few films from the 1930s, when a gangster needs to talk business with his dinner guest, he asks the ladies to **take a powder**. Most students of vernacular speech reject the bathroom break as the origin of the phrase, pointing out that *powder* was used colloquially as a verb as far back as the seventeenth century, when it meant to *make haste*. The minor poet Francis Quarles (1592–1644) wrote this in his *Divine Fancies* of 1632: "Zacheus climb'd the Tree: But O how fast . . . (when Our Saviour called) he **powder'd** down agen!" About the same time, *dust* was used similarly as a verb, meaning to go very quickly, raising a cloud of dust. Presumably, *powder* was used descriptively as the equivalent of *dust*. Thus, to **take a**

powder meant to leave so hurriedly that one raised a cloud of dust.

Or did it? Although the equation of *powder* and *dust* does fit nicely with the notion of a speedy departure, the action actually conveyed by the phrase is to *take* a powder, not to *raise* or *stir up* or *create* or even *leave* a powder, which is what happens when a fleeing person raises a powdery cloud of dust. Although the word *powder* in connection with haste appears in seventeenth-century English poetry, the phrase **take a powder** does not appear in a U.S. source until May 20, 1916, in the *Washington Post*: "Look at the two birds trying to take a run-out powder on the eats." The highly colloquial sentence is a bit cryptic, but may be translated into conventional English this way: "Look at the two deadbeat guys (see **bird**) trying to skip out without paying the check for their meal (the *eats*)." Note also that the phrase used is "a run-out powder," which occurs in other early uses of the expression. This is key. In the late nineteenth and early twentieth century, patent medicines generally came in two forms, liquid or powder. Pills, which were generally hand-rolled by a doctor or pharmacist, were rare, and capsules were a later development. To dose yourself with medicine was to **take a powder**. The most common patent medicines were, in fact, varieties of laxatives—the belief being that constipation was the cause of most complaints. A laxative was a **run-out powder**: Take it, and you had to run out. The most likely source of the expression to **take a powder**, therefore, is the practice of self-medicating with a laxative, which leaves one no choice but to run out.

Talkin' through your hat—You are exaggerating or lying. The expression has been in use since at least the early 1900s and remained popular until the mid-1960s, when hats went out of fashion (at least for men). The phrase suggests the image of covert conversation, in which the speaker puts his hat over his face. Many authorities believe the expression grew out of disingenuous worshippers in church, who conducted conversations "through their hats" (with the hat covering the face) under pretense of prayer. *See* **Don't hand me that line!**

Throw your mother a bone!—You are a son of a bitch (literally). Reported by Eric Partridge as being from the 1930s, this is an indirect yet vivid way of simultaneously insulting a person and his mother. See also, **Your mother wears army shoes**.

Two-timer—One who deceives and betrays; a cheater on one's girlfriend or boyfriend. The word may come from the notion of two-at-a-time or from "making time" (making out, making love) with two people at once.

Up your tail with a rusty nail!—A mild curse or a "friendly" toast, as in: "Ladies and gentlemen, raise your glasses to our guest of honor, please. Your Eminence, it is a privilege to have you with us. **Up your tail with a rusty nail!**" "**Up your nose with a rubber hose**" is an even more familiar variation. Both catchphrases were current during the 1920s, Prohibition paradoxically creating a high demand for "clever" toasts.

Voulez-vous squattez-vous?–Ostensibly an invitation to sit down, but by World War II frequently meaning, *Do you need to use the toilet?* Although this faux French phrase enjoyed bursts of popularity after both world wars, its origin lies in the 1820s, when **Voulez-vous squattez-vous?** was a gag line coined by the Great Grimaldi (Joseph Grimaldi, 1778–1837), the most famous clown in early nineteenth-century London.

Wake up and smell the coffee!—Stop being naïve; face facts. Because the phrase apparently appeared during the "Golden Age" of television—the early to mid-1950s—some students of American slang believe it originated in an advertising slogan. Popular historians, however, have been unable to identify anything of the kind. "Oh, **wake up and smell the coffee!** I don't care who he says he's been writing those checks to. Your husband does not have an 'internist' named Boom-Boom."

Ward heeler—A local political functionary or hack; a low-level operative for a political boss. The implication is that this is a corrupt person operating in a corrupt political system. The term was born during the heyday of New York's Tammany Hall in the nineteenth century and resurfaced in a big way during the exuberantly corrupt urban politics of the Prohibition era (1920s). The **ward heeler** tramps through ("heels") his assigned ward (city precinct or neighborhood), soliciting bribes, collecting bribes, and conveying orders from on high. The word *heeler* may also suggest the obedient behavior of a dog who invariably heels at his master's command.

Weak sister—A timid, cowardly, vacillating, unreliable man; the weak link on a team or in an organization. The phrase has been in use since the mid-nineteenth century but resurfaced with a vengeance in the 1910s and 1920s, especially to describe an inept member of a team or other enterprise whose anxiety and uncertainty threatened the morale of the entire organization. The reemergence of the phrase in the first quarter of the twentieth century may have been linked to the rise of the term **sob sister**, first used in 1912 to describe a newspaper reporter or columnist who specializes in writing hyper-sentimental *sob stories*. Such journalism became especially popular in the decade following World War I.

Weirdo—A strange person whose nonconformity is perceived as disturbing and repellant. The word emerged in the 1940s, when the urgent pressures of a world war put a high premium on social conformity (everyone doing his bit) even while it created stresses that provoked some individuals to behavior perceived as weird. Variations include **weirdie** and **weirdy**.

Wet blanket—*The Oxford English Dictionary*, which defines the phrase as "a person who has a depressing or dispiriting effect on those around him," finds the earliest example of its use in 1857. The phrase was uttered a great deal during the 1920s, an era of frenetic boosterism and forced optimism. "When you lose a bet, it's time to double down! Stop being such a **wet blanket**!" The term is derived from the practice of putting out a cooking or campfire with a water-soaked blanket. It extinguishes the flame.

What gives?—What's going on? The very first appearance of this uniquely American expression was in *Pal Joey*, the 1940 story by John O'Hara (1905–1970). Most linguists believe that it is a translation of Yiddish (perhaps German) *Was gibt?* (What's going on?). Wherever it comes from, it is a vintage tough-guy demand for an explanation. "I heard you were with another fella, Babs. **What gives?**"

Work both sides of the street—Be duplicitous; have it both ways. Today, the meaning of this phrase is to be two-faced or to try to have your cake and eat it too. In the 1930s, when the phrase was more frequently heard, its meaning may have been closer to its origin, which was almost certainly in the informal agreements beggars, apple sellers, and the like made for the division of their territory: One man would work one side of the street, another would confine himself to the other side, and neither would intrude on the other's territory. **To work both sides of the street**, therefore, was in this sense less about being duplicitous or two-faced than it was about being piggy.

Worrywart—A chronically anxious person who frets about virtually everything. On March 20, 1922, the Canadian-born U.S. cartoonist J. R. Williams (1888–1957) debuted *Out Our Way,* a newspaper comic strip depicting rural and small-town life. The strip caught on and was eventually syndicated in some seven hundred papers, appearing through 1977, having outlived its creator by two decades. One of the many characters featured throughout the years was an eight-year-old boy known only as The Worry Wort. Very popular (the Worry Wort starred in his own comic book in 1956), this character seems to have been the source for the expression.

Yeah, you could shit a brick—Like hell you could. An expression that comes straight from the gut, circa 1930. "Get a bank to loan *you* money. **Yeah, you could shit a brick**."

Your mother wears army shoes (or **boots**)— Today, a jocular and mildly derisive way of dismissing someone or something someone says: "You're going to vote for *that* idiot? **Aw, your mother wears army shoes**." When originally introduced, during World War II, the implication was far more insulting: If your mother wears army shoes, she must be sleeping with soldiers. In other words, *your mother's a whore*. Variations include **Your sister wears army shoes** (or **boots**), **Your mother eats K rations**, and **your mother drives a tank**. Many expressions go out of style, become obsolete, or are simply forgotten; this one is a rare instance of the semantic evolutionary process known as amelioration, by which a highly insulting expression mellows overtime, becoming harmless and even vaguely nonsensical.

You're not the only pebble on the beach—A classic deflator best wielded by a real prick. Probably born at the end of the nineteenth century, the phrase was used through at least the 1930s. The object of this expression is to reduce the hearer to the insignificance he or she merits with a figure of speech that defines all humanity as pretty much equally insignificant:

Liver-spotted butcher (in mid-cleaver stroke) to impatient customer in line: "Take a number, mister. **You're not the only pebble on the beach**."

Zhlub—A slob, boor (Yiddish). Another Yiddish borrowing, in with the tide of immigration from Central and Eastern Europe at the end of the nineteenth century. The word is very derisive, but also implies that the person cannot help himself—as attested to by the fact that, quite often, the adjective *poor* precedes **zhlub**: "The poor **zhlub** just didn't know any better."